LIVING IN THE NEW PARADIGM

Consciously co-creating our new reality

Lead author

Laura Billingham

THE BOOK CHIEF®

IGNITE YOUR WRITING

Table of Contents

Foreword

by Dillon Dhanecha

In an epoch of the human existence poised on the brink of profound change for the individual and the collective, this book emerges as a clarion call to reimagine our collective destiny.

It draws from the wellspring of a vision conceived in 2021 by Laura Billingham, its lead author—a vision that is as formidable as it is exhilarating.

Providing a platform for previously quiet voices to emerge as beacons of light, this vision of human evolution has its genesis in the truth that wisdom and change often emerge fro those the world least expects.

Laura's initial hesitation mirrors the collective self-doubt so many of us face when called to catalysing the shift in global shift in consciousness.

As a true inspiration to us all, the persistence of her vision and the realisation of this manuscript symbolises the transformative power of inner truth that needs only the veil of fear to be lifted.

In the journey from self-doubt to self-realisation, Laura herself embodies the very essence of how divine feminine and divine masculine must integrate to provide the foundation on which any new paradigm for our human experience must be built.

In this coming together of solar and lunar energies, Laura beautifully plants the seed of "we can" in the hearts of all who read the words that follow.

What you hold in your hands then is not simply a book but a manifesto, a symphony of voices united by the audacious belief that we can co-create a brighter world.

It stands as a testament to the power of human imagination and the resilience of those who dare to dream beyond the confines of the present.

Each chapter in this volume, authored by a diverse group of thinkers and dreamers, offers a unique lens on what it means to live in the new paradigm.

These narratives range from pragmatic shifts in governance and healthcare to utopian visions of a society in harmony with nature, all underscored by a collective vision very much resonant with teachings from A Course in Miracles:

"Miracles occur naturally as expressions of love. The real miracle is the love that inspires them."

This book extends that profound wisdom, emphasising the real transformation that begins with and is held by unwavering love for people, planet, flora and fauna.

This isn't just a collection of futuristic essays; it's a mosaic of heartfelt desires of people who envision a world characterised by unity, by love, by compassion and most of all by our humanity.

Furthermore, this endeavour challenges us to transcend the paradigms created by our primitive survival wiring and break out of the human experience rooted in fear and scarcity that we endure today.

It invites us to awaken the dormant superhuman powers within each of us—capacities for extraordinary compassion, deep intuition, creative innovation, heightened sensory and non-sensory perception that can only be put to work by a consciousness unshackled by fear.

These are the tools with which we can forge a new paradigm for a highly evolved species.

The authors in this book are not merely contributors as much as they are heralds of a new age.

They remind us that the path to a more evolved society requires a significant paradigm shift.

As you engage with this book, let it ignite your imagination and inspire you to consider your role in this transformative journey to the new paradigm.

Most of all, take the call to contribute to this tapestry of change through your own thoughts, dreams, and actions.

Allow the boldness of this vision to move you, the depth of its wisdom to guide you and the purity of its intent to inspire you.

Together, armed with the knowledge of our past and the dreams of our future, we can create a world that reflects our highest aspirations.

In the spirit of "A million dreams" from The Last Showman, this book beckons you to be part of something monumental, to dream a new world into being.

7

If there was ever a time to imagine a new paradigm for the future, that time would be now.

Our time is indeed, now.

Dillon Dhanecha Bio

Dillon is the kind of human that doesn't fit categories. Equal parts multi-millionaire social housing investor and international spiritual teacher, he has built a property portfolio to house vulnerable people, launched Europe's only Gold Bullion Buying Club to make the shiny stuff available to everyday people and created a proprietary energy healing modality using principles of neuro-yogic science that has given him the accolade of being "Joe Dispenza on steroids". By his own admission, an unlikely mix of activity that helps him to explore the wonders of a material world built around the money game through a deeply spiritual and philanthropic lens.

http://www.lucidape.link/

Note from the lead author

I first imagined creating this book back in 2021 – some would say I received a download, an instruction to gather humanity together to dream a new world into existence. The concept felt "too big" – what business did a late 50s woman have in believing such a thing could even happen?

Who did I think I was?

And so the idea was shelved in my head…

But it wouldn't let go of me.

It nagged and niggled at me.

The title was on a loop in my mind, and then the subheading wrote itself.

I created the concept for the cover.

It started to feel real – as if it were already written.

Slowly I found other dreamers who wanted to take part – not as many as I would have liked, and yet I know why people were loath to come forward, this is uncharted water, and initially only the brave, the risk-takers, the biggest dreamers could understand the concept.

By the late summer of 2023, I had enough people to make the book a possibility – and a tentative release date of Jan 2024 was mooted. But something was wrong. The energy of January just wasn't working for me. Why launch a book about the possibilities of a new and brighter future in the darkest, most depressing month of the year?

The astrologer, Sam Selby, looked at the heavens for me and a revised date of May 2024 was set. Sam was going to feature in the book, but sadly, personal circumstances stood in her way.

Strangely (or not!) this new May date energised the contributors who began to submit their chapters…and what chapters they were (or rather "they are").

Read on, and prepare to add your own dreams to the mix…

To quote the song from "The Last Showman" - *"A million dreams is what it's going to take."*

Introduction

The phrase "new paradigm" has been bandied about for several years now, but what does it mean?

I suppose the answer to that question depends on who you ask! For some people, it will mean absolutely nothing, nada, zilch. For others, it is simply another "buzzword" that is touted by a bunch of new agers. Yet others may resonate with the phrase without really knowing why.

And then there are those of us who truly believe there is a better way for all of us to exist on this beautiful planet we call home – Earth. To us, living in the new paradigm means moving away from the ways of living perpetuated in modern day (Western) societies across the globe, and into a newer, gentler way, that is more in tune with our bodies and the planet that sustains us.

Each of the co-authors has written about their particular slant on this new paradigm lifestyle. Some have taken the very pragmatic approach of writing about the actual changes to governance, medicine, agriculture, etc., that they would like to see. Others have quite literally, "dreamt" of a better way, and written about that.

I believe if we can think, dream, or imagine something, that "thing" can be made reality. As Napolean Hill wrote in 1937 in his seminal book "Think and Grow Rich"… "thoughts are things, and powerful things at that, when they are mixed with definiteness of purpose, persistence, and a BURNING DESIRE for their translation into riches, or other material objects."

Napoleon Hill may have been mainly concerned with growing wealthy, but, to my mind, if enough of us can think / dream / imagine a better, more sustainable future, AND work towards it, even if only in tiny increments, we can bring this better future – the new paradigm – into existence.

Woo-woo, perhaps, but in the 19th century, mobile telephones, computers, space travel, TV, in fact all the technology we now perceive as normal, would have been regarded as miraculous and impossible.

And all the tech we now take for granted was first a dream, a thought, in someone's mind.

If someone can imagine and describe a way of communicating that doesn't require cables and wires, why can't someone else imagine a world where energy is free and drawn from the air?

Tesla did.

The reason mobile telephony succeeded and "free energy" did not, is the 1%ers who currently control the world would not make a profit out of free energy!

My own chapter, which follows immediately after this intro, is my personal vision of the future. It is a story, an imagining…because that's the way my brain operates. Other authors have been very specific, and analytical, and others very spiritual. And yet, I discovered when reading all the chapters, there is one underlying theme: LOVE.

Love of the planet, love of humanity, love of each other…I did not expect that, although perhaps I should have – and somehow it seems entirely appropriate. For after all, the highest vibrational energy of them all is love, and it is precisely what is required to heal the planet and, in turn, humanity.

After each of the chapters, I have included some of my thoughts – except on my own…that would be too weird, even for me!

I would invite you to do the same. When you read each chapter, take a few notes. What resonated strongly with you? What did you agree with, and what made you shake your head negatively?

Do you have your own ideas about our New Paradigm and would you like to share them in a second volume? If the answer is YES, please contact me, Laura Billingham, at **hello@word-witch.co.uk**.

And finally, enjoy the book, it has been a long time in the making!

Chapter 1

After the End

By Laura Billingham

My name is Elodia, I am 97 years old, and I was born 250 years after "the end". As I am now in the latter part of my life – although I still hope to see another 40 years or more – I have begun to think about what came before.

They (whoever "they" are) say the world had to burn down in order for those that remained to rebuild it in a better way. I'm not sure I entirely agree with this. Perhaps it should have been possible to dismantle the old systems and start anew; many more of my species would have survived...as well as the wondrous buildings and cities I have read about.

But we will never know, and the wonders of the past remain only in the memory banks of our quantum computers; available to view and experience in holographic form only.

All the history texts tell us the old paradigm was a cruel and violent place to live. Wars raged incessantly around the globe. Profit was more important than people. The land was raped. The seas and rivers polluted. Individuality reigned over collaboration. The strongest, most aggressive, least empathic humans kept the rest of the world enslaved and trapped in a matrix of their design.

Mother Earth wept.

Father Sky mourned.

And yet, in the 21st Century, some people around the world were beginning to wake up, realise what was happening, and choose to disconnect from what they perceived as a false paradigm – some even used the term "matrix".

These souls were the ancestors of everyone who now remain – less than 2 billion people now occupy a world that once hosted 8 billion or more, and the Earth flourishes again.

The almost total annihilation of what once was, allowed for a complete rework of society and its structures. With no banking system, the power of money and profit was reduced to almost zero, those who had survived with monetary wealth in the form of notes and currency, soon found that it was useless in a new world that valued food production over the bottom line. If they couldn't collaborate with those who grew and manufactured food, they quickly realised they would not eat. I'm told that bank notes (I've only seen images) were often used in lieu of kindling in the early days of the reimagining of the world, their value being perceived more in what they were useful for than in what they used to be able to buy.

Survivors of the destruction tended to be in the less densely populated and rural areas of the old world. Places to where many people had already escaped in order to break free of the matrix imposed upon and around them. The survivors were already ahead of the game when it came to reestablishing a new society…a new paradigm.

After "the end", freed of societal constraints as to what could, or could not, be achieved, scientific breakthroughs of staggering potential began to be made, the most important of which was the rediscovery of the works of Nikola Tesla around gathering energy from the cosmos.

Within 10 years of the annihilation, everyone on the planet had access to free and unlimited energy, and communication networks spanned the globe. Great leaps were made in the field of molecular science, allowing for the manipulation of energy into matter…housing, clothing, furniture, all can be created from seemingly "thin air".

Once used, or no longer wanted, everything can be broken back down to a molecular level and recycled into something else.

Learning from the past, knowledge is now freely shared, no licenses are ever granted, so no one company or individual can profit from innovation. If someone wants more, a bigger house, new clothes, they can create it with no need to pay a third party.

With no need for money, and unlimited resources, people can be whoever they want to be. They can choose if they want to train in medicine, arts, literature, science, without being motivated by the potential financial reward.

Added to this, technology has advanced, so that what were once thought of as "menial jobs" can be performed by robotic creations. Working is all about what is meaningful to an individual. Some people choose never to work at all, being content to live each day as they wish. The only obligation for these individuals is to commit to a minimum of eight hours' work per week to the community farms and fisheries. If they refuse, they are unable to access fresh organic produce and instead rely on synthetically replicated food. Perfectly nutritious, just not fresh from the planet.

Many people back in the early days did choose this route. To some, it was the easy way and, if that was their decision, it was respected by the rest of the population.

Most people, however, grew to love the feel of soil on their hands, and indeed many chose to create their own small holdings and live entirely from the land – much as their very early ancestors had done millennia ago. Of course, the perils of the past, of crop failure, disease, poor weather conditions, were mitigated by the fact that the new farmers could always fall back on replicated food if they needed to. Add to this advances in hydroponics and actually it is easy to keep the population well fed and well nourished. There are no ultra-processed foods – people cook from fresh for their family, or join community kitchens and eat with a group.

With fewer humans to defile her, Mother Earth was reborn, although it took several generations for the pollution and contamination of the end of days to dissipate. Where once large cities had flourished and ultimately failed, park and farmland took over; all over the Earth, concrete and brick were replaced by greenery, and trees. With no artificial chemical fertilisers being used on the land, there was no runoff into waterways, and the rivers, streams and oceans became clear and clean once more. Fish stocks replenished, and our mammalian cousins – dolphins and whales – repopulated the seas.

I grew up on a smallholding with my parents and siblings in the early part of the 24th century. We raised our own pigs and chickens and grew much of our own fruit and vegetables. Everything else we needed came from the community farms where each of us worked at least one day a week – usually more. It was a very happy, fulfilled childhood. We were at one with nature - in fact, we knew no other way than to listen to the cycles of the Earth and our own bodies.

Educating children had stopped being enforced and regimented long before I was born, instead every child is encouraged to find their own path in life.

Nurseries and kindergartens now abound where children can learn if they wish, or play if that is their preference. Over the years, it became obvious that small children are, in the main, keen to learn new things; removing the rote learning of the past simply allows a child to develop at a pace that is right for them. "School years" don't exist, instead a bright child of four, could be "taught" alongside ten year olds; as long as all benefit, age is not a barrier to learning.

I chose to attend school regularly and discovered an ability to heal, so I trained as a medic, using natural methods to help my patients. During the course of my training, science discovered that something mooted back in the 21st century – namely that humanity should have 12 strand DNA – was in fact the truth.

Some of us, including my family, have already attained this evolutionary step and we have certain abilities our antecedents could only dream off…you could call them superpowers.

Some of us are telepathic, some, like me, can heal through touch and sound, others are able to physically relocate themselves and other things using only the power of their mind, and yet others are able to encourage plant growth. Would this evolution have happened in the old world? Who knows? It may already have been happening before the world burned, those with the potential to move to 12 Strand DNA were probably the ones who began to disconnect from 21st century indoctrination and that may explain why so many in this age possess the new DNA – we inherited it from our forebears.

As I reread the words I have just written, I wonder that this way of living wasn't always in existence.

What happened that caused mankind to deviate so far from the natural world during the 20th and 21st centuries?

I can only conclude that there must have been some kind of collective blindness to what was going on, and that the quest for power and wealth by a small minority held the rest of the world in a death grip, seemingly unable to see an alternative. Great advances in technology in the 20th century were not used for the good of all, but for the benefit of the few. Geniuses like Tesla were ridiculed by those desperate to protect their own power and wealth. Governments and large corporations lined their own pockets, leaving little for the general population.

Ordinary people lived with a scarcity consciousness whilst all the while the rich got richer, hoarding their wealth and refusing to share the bounty of the world.

It makes no sense to me, and yet it happened, and kept happening for centuries.

I pray we have changed enough as a species to never allow the mistakes of the past to infect the present and the future. As we travel amongst the galaxies meeting new civilisations and learning more about the Universe, I feel most of us now understand and believe in the phrase…

"Everything is the all, and the all is everything."

We are all connected to the planet, the Universe, and each other. No one is separate, everyone is part of The All.

And I am profoundly glad to live in this New Paradigm.

Chapter 2

A New Paradigm in the Future of Work

by Amanda Cookson

Introduction

As a child, I was steeped in a world where the impossible seemed possible. This unconventional upbringing, once a source of embarrassment, became the bedrock of my business ethos: embracing change and challenging old paradigms.

My mother lived next door to Veteran ufologist Denis Plunkett, founder of the British Flying Saucer Bureau. I think having conversations about aliens from a young age created her open-minded attitude and passion for the new age.

I had an unconventional childhood; I grew up in a haunted house with a family that believed in magical thinking. For weekends we would visit new age fairs and wander local woodlands looking for signs of the little folk. If anything was lost, we would dowse for it; if I was ill, my mother would realign my energies. Metaphysics, remote viewing and the power of positive thinking were all a part of our everyday conversations.

We were weird and when I was younger, weird was something to hide rather than celebrate. So I ignored and dismissed much of the thinking I was brought up with. When I established my own coaching business, things began to change.

Travelling home from a Do Lectures event holding on to my James Victore 'Stay Weird' bag, I started to explore all the weird experiences that uniquely shaped my thinking.

I started to see in myself and my clients how your mindset, energies and model of the world impact on your life experiences.

"Alice had begun to think that very few things indeed were really impossible."

Alice's Adventures in Wonderland

-Lewis Carroll-

The new paradigm I describe in this chapter I believe is already here in some outlier businesses and thinkers. In this chapter, I will outline the 3 hypotheses my business is based on and why our clients are enjoying extraordinary results through this new thinking. My hope is that the ideas we share will continue catalysing a movement that is bringing about a new paradigm in the world of work.

Old belief: You can't teach an old dog new tricks

New paradigm: Everyone can change

I trained as a teacher in the 80s. We were taught that your brain stops developing when you reach 25 years of age and slowly goes into decline as we deteriorate into old age. No new cells can be created: you can't teach an old dog new tricks.

With understanding from neuroscience, we now know that our brain is constantly evolving; and adapts, reshapes, and rewires itself to better suit the tasks we perform.

For example, research found that London taxi drivers have an enlarged hippocampus, why? - because this is the brain region that supports navigation. As taxi drivers learn 'the knowledge', their brain adapts to support them.

My business is founded on the belief that everyone can change. We are not fixed by our circumstances. We can learn new skills and develop new neural pathways. Our behaviour is not fixed. With time, motivation and support, any change we seek is possible for us.

When you believe everyone can change, you are living in a paradigm where change is possible for all, including yourself and the people around you.

Carol Dweck's work on the growth mindset emerged from her research into what were the key factors for students getting into the top schools in America. She was interested in understanding why children with the highest IQs weren't always the most successful. What she discovered was that your mental attitude was more important than the intellect you had inherited. Those with a growth mindset who saw mistakes as learning and effort as the reason for their success got into better schools than those who saw their intelligence as fixed.

Put simply, your attitude creates your success.

Researchers found that when children tackled an unsolvable problem, they persisted longer and felt no shame in not completing the task when they approached it from a 'super hero's' mindset. e.g. 'What would Batman do?'.

The growth mindset is now taught in workplaces and schools across the world. Contributing to a new paradigm where success is about effort and learning, which supports a belief that everyone can change.

I am seeing more organisations moving away from authoritative or charismatic leadership figures to developing leaders who can become enablers of growth and development.

What does this look like in my work as a coach?

As a coach, I have noticed that the extent to which people can change is down to their belief system.

"Whether you think you can, or you think you can't, you're right."

-Henry Ford-

When we are in a victim mindset. We perceive everything as being done to us and we are powerless to influence. When we shift into a space of self-empowerment, we can see the opportunities for change are in front of us. Often my work is centred on spotting the limiting beliefs and assumptions that are getting in the way of change and then helping clients identify what changes they can make to their choices and behaviour to get the results they want.

In the new paradigm, everyone knows they are never stuck, they can change their choices and when they do, those different choices create different results.

Want to step into this new paradigm?

1.Read this statement:

Who I am is not fixed, I am a work in progress. If I am not happy with my circumstances, I can learn to do things differently and change my results.

Write down your reactions: how you feel, what do you agree with, and what do you object to?

In your objections lie the work you need to do to create change for yourself.

2. Answer this question:

If anything was possible for you, what would you do?

What first step would you take?

Old belief: Emotion has no place at work

New Paradigm: How it feels at work matters

When I first started work, I was told to 'leave my personality at the door'. Leadership was highly directive, and employee conformity and compliance were prized. The focus was on tasks and productivity. Much thinking in my early career was on efficiencies: how can we do tasks as quickly as possible?

Today's workplace is very different. The pace of change is rapid and most industries have experienced disruption. This increasing level of complexity means the future is unpredictable and the problems we are facing at work need a different approach. Increasingly, employees are being asked to collaborate with a wide diversity of thinkers, often across dispersed locations, and solve problems that no-one has ever faced before. In order to do this, we, as human beings, need to be able to unlock our best thinking.

How it feels at work matters because of the way our brain works. There is increased evidence that how we feel as human beings influences our ability to think and work effectively.

Neuroscientists have discovered that when human beings are stressed or under threat, the level of a brain chemical called cortisol rises in our system and our ability to access the part of our brain that does our best innovative, creative thinking shuts off.

In this stressed state, we become reactive, are more pessimistic, drop in IQ, make more errors, and are less able to collaborate or think innovatively.

"We like to think we are rational beings who occasionally have emotions, but actually… we are emotional, feeling beings; who, on rare occasions, think." Dr Brené Brown.

The best way to help people to access their whole brain, innovate and solve complex problems is to work in an environment that is 'psychologically safe'.

Psychological safety is an atmosphere of high trust where it feels safe to express your opinions; ask for and share feedback; and offer ideas and observations without fear of upsetting others or negative judgement.

"People may forget what you said, but will never forget how you made them feel."

-Maya Angelou-

When psychological safety is not there, mistakes are made, businesses fail, and lives are lost.

As an example, healthcare is the 3rd biggest cause of death in America, with over 400,000 preventable deaths each year. To help solve this problem, Teodor Grantcharov was inspired by the black box technology used in aviation and created a black box for the Operating Room. Rather than being a box, it is a series of sensors that monitor activities across the OR. Currently, his system uses AI and processes 1 million data points a day. Through this research, they discovered changing how comfortable it felt in the OR for people to communicate was key in saving lives.

Teams with low psychological safety were less likely to share ideas, offer feedback, and raise issues.

Leaders wanting to create a psychologically safe environment need to do two key things.

Lead in a brain friendly way that is empowering, motivational and encourages high levels of learning, innovation and productivity.

Regulate their emotions so they are not yelling or behaving in a way that elevates the threat response in others.

The old paradigm called for the suppression of emotion behind a professional facade. Suppression involves masking how we are feeling, putting on a brave face, and pretending everything is 'FINE' when it isn't. Research has now linked an increased risk of heart disease to people who tend to suppress their feelings. Bottling our feelings up whether we are at work or at home is not good for our health and has been linked in further studies to relationship issues and lower levels of likability.

The healthiest way to manage emotion is to use the appraisal technique. To do this, in the moment, rather than suppress the feeling, focus on your thinking about the feelings you are having. Label your experience, rather than say 'I am angry' and make the emotion a loss of your identity say 'I am experiencing the sensation of anger' - this labelling and distancing will help you gain more control and see your choices in the emotion rather than being triggered by it.

For more on this technique, see the section below headed: Want to step into this new paradigm?

The more leaders, managers and individuals learn how to manage with emotion, the healthier we will be as a society.

How it feels at work matters because how we are allowed to express and manage our emotions affects memory, learning, relationships, health and if that's not enough to persuade you, could even impact world peace.

A nationwide survey of Jewish-Israeli adults during the Gaza War discovered that those who self-reported using appraisal techniques to regulate their negative emotions were more supportive of providing humanitarian aid than those who didn't use reappraisal techniques.

This research was tested again using randomised Israeli participants. Findings indicated that participants trained to use reappraisal showed greater support for conciliatory policies and these effects were still evident five months after the training.

"Leadership is not about being in charge. It's about taking care of those in your charge."

-Simon Sinek-

What does this look like in my work as a coach?

Much of what people talk about in coaching are the difficult conversations and emotions that spring up at work. The things that they can't talk about eat away at them and many people now find themselves at risk of burnout because they are unable to communicate how they feel.

In the new paradigm, everyone would have the right to work in a psychologically safe environment where they can express their truths and be their authentic self. The more people who learn how to create safe environments and regulate their emotions, the more positively they will impact society.

Want to step into this new paradigm?

To help yourself, practise reappraisal.

When you next experience an emotion you don't like, change your self-talk by using this 3-step mindful self-compassion technique.

Step 1: Notice the emotion

When you notice the emotion, say to yourself: Noticing this emotion is mindfulness

Step 2: Express humanity

Take a moment to recognise that experiencing emotions both good and bad is a part of being a human being. Getting cross, feeling anxious, whatever it is, it's all normal.

Step 3: Offer Self Compassion

Place your hand on your body where it feels most soothing and talk to yourselves like you would a friend. e.g. It's OK, you are going to be OK. You are doing your best.

Old belief: Sticks and stones may break my bones, but names will never hurt me.

New Belief: Words create worlds.

As a child of the 70s, I grew up with the phrase 'sticks and stones may break my bones, but names will never hurt me'. The 'politically correct' brigade were battling against the passive racism and misogyny that were rife in our everyday language and popular culture. Opponents would scoff - what difference does it make if I call this a black mark or call someone a dolly bird?

40 years on, we know we think in metaphors and that the language we use makes a world of difference in what people think is possible for them.

The work of neuroscientist Matt Leiberman has identified that we experience social pain in the same parts of our brain as physical pain. Social pain can be verbal attacks, or when people are shamed, belittled, bullied or shunned. Social pain is felt when it is either a direct attack on us or observed with others.

This knowledge creates the new paradigm where we choose our language with care. When we know that our words can destroy another person's confidence, limit their thinking, create mistrust and increase separation; we will speak with compassion and care.

Anyone familiar with manifesting will also know how our words can create. A clear intention can focus the mind and attract positive outcomes. What we may not have realised is how the words we say to ourselves and to others are also creating the world around us.

In 2016, I trained with the late Judith E Glaser, creator of Conversational Intelligence. The body of her work was based on the neuroscience of conversations and how the words you use in conversations will either elevate levels of oxytocin and create connection and encourage collaboration, or elevate cortisol and generate mistrust and disconnection.

Building high trust relationships and a deeper connection with others can be learned.

In the new paradigm, people can express their needs and get them met by others because they are able to articulate their thoughts and feelings in a way that boosts oxytocin.

We feel safe with others, we feel seen and because of this, more and more of us are moving out of survival mode and looking to explore higher levels of thinking.

What does this look like in my work as a coach?

Increasing numbers of leaders are looking to learn coach-like behaviours. To create a listening space and ask questions that open up new ideas and generate higher levels of performance.

"To get a better life you need to ask better questions."

-Tony Robbins-

Want to step into this new paradigm?

You can have more oxytocin boosting green conversations with other people by doing these three things:

Listening without interruption or judgement. When we give people the gift of our presence and listen to them without judgement or distraction, magic happens.

People value being listened to. There is no need to jump into fixing mode, or worry about saying something clever, just listen.

Mirroring - this is a technique used in empathetic listening where you pose the exact word or phrase said back to the person who said it as a question.

E.g. They say, 'I am feeling flustered'. And you say - 'So you are feeling flustered?'

This works because when we hear our words played back to us, we know the other person is listening and it helps us feel seen, plus hearing our words can prompt better thinking.

Curiosity - when we stay in an open and curious frame of mind, we are more likely to discover new ideas and approaches. By being curious, we demonstrate an appreciation for others' thinking.

E.g. If someone says something you don't agree with or is left field; you say, 'That's interesting, I had not thought about it that way - can you tell me more about that or - can you help me understand your thinking?'

Changing the world one conversation at a time

I have pointed my attention to the workplace because the big global forces of power are mostly interested in commerce. When new thinking has a positive impact on business success, it is more likely to be adopted. How we feel and behave at work impacts and influences how we feel and behave at home. What the government feels is the right training and mindset for the world of work influences learning at school. When schools and workplaces support new thinking, society pivots.

In each of the three areas, everyone can change. How it feels at work matters, and words create worlds; there is a positive impact on individuals, workplaces and humanity as a whole. I hope you will join me in making this new paradigm a reality.

In my new paradigm, people are self-aware, able to express themselves in nonviolent ways that boost connection and trust. Our schools, parenting and workplaces are brain friendly environments where we work together to solve problems.

"Your life is a reflection of your thoughts. If you change your thinking, you change your life."

-Brian Tracy-

Note by the lead author

What I love about Amanda's contribution is how she learned to embrace what she used to think of as her "weird upbringing".

Being brought up as a child in a haunted house, next door to a ufologist, with a family who "believed in magical thinking", sounds like the kind of childhood I would have adored. My parents were pretty open minded, and encouraged free thinking, but the "weirdest" they got was leaving copies of Erich von Daniken books around! Books I obviously read I should add.

Amanda now runs a successful business coaching practice using concepts that used to be seen as being "too soft, too rooted in feelings and emotions". As Amanda says, we are used to the "suppression of emotion behind a professional façade" concept that most (if not all) of us grew up. The idea that we shouldn't utilise the emotional and feeling side of ourselves at work became (and still is in many sectors) the absolute norm and it's great to see that Amanda, and others like her, are successfully overturning this old paradigm way of business and work.

Being the dreamer that I am, my New Paradigm imagines humans working only in roles and occupations that fulfil them, with many tasks being performed by technology.

Whilst respecting the fact that most of us do need to have some kind of purpose in our lives, and for many, that is "work", I don't believe that we should have to engage in occupations that destroy our soul and sense of self, especially if something exists that can perform the jobs we don't want to do!

In the current paradigm, we work to survive, pay our bills, get by, whilst a tiny minority profit from our efforts. Imagine how much more fulfilling all our lives could be if the "profit for a few" model wasn't the driving force behind businesses. If we all had access to everything we need. If we could all work jobs that made our hearts sing…

I'll close with a quote from Amanda:

"How it feels at work matters, and words create worlds"

Chapter 3

Release the trauma, release the world: An exploration

by Andrea Hochgatterer

Unravel the thread and spin a new story:

Part One:

Where are we now?

The world we live in nowadays, particularly in our western civilisation, seems to me incapable of calming down. Instead of making people feel secure, protected, happily productive and fulfilled in their life, our so called developed world acts as a collective mind with traits similar to an A-Type personality, with the predominant features of "not being good enough" as we are.

We are collectively told we have to be more, be better, be richer than we were yesterday. Everyday improving, stepping it up, reaching yet another goal, aiming for something better, more exciting, more expensive. Industries are producing an ever increasing amount of goods, which are virtually identical, to ensure that productivity is on the up, and alongside this, more jobs are created; however, profits are not passed on and instead companies are required to make more and more money. The accumulation of wealth is the new god for some, however, this wealth is not available to others.

A-type personality traits, as we know, are based on a learned behaviour from our peers, and at times are the causes for ACE (Adverse Childhood Experience) trauma, impacting a child overburdened by demands and expectations which it could not meet, and leaving behind a lifelong struggle for self-acceptance and fulfilment.

This model of society, commerce and economy impacts everybody's daily lives; their thinking, their beliefs and values; the constant striving for betterment will be or already is, unsustainable in the long term, particularly in the face of poverty, starvation and the suppression of personal rights in many parts of the world. Not to mention the impact it has on our health and wellbeing.

Fear, anxiety and mental problems are on a steady rise, health systems are failing, global warming, energy crisis, job losses, the gap between the ultra-rich and poorer populations is forever on the increase. We are still waging wars against each other, nation against nation, peoples against peoples, person against person.

But why?

To come to a better understanding, let's start unravelling the thread:

Society stands again like so many times before, at the cusp of a new development, a rise in understanding and awareness, however, this new consciousness, of which I can see glimmers of hope shining through the fabric of our society, is not enough to facilitate a major shift to a globally humane way of living where all and everything is being considered globally for the betterment of our world, of mother earth inclusive of all its creatures, inclusive of the whole universe.

Unfortunately, we are seemingly performing a constant tug of war in which we are individually and globally pulling in different directions, causing deeper and deeper rifts which separate us from each other and from our innermost self, preventing a harmonious development for everyone, just when we need a world whose paradigms are finally shifting faster than ever, in order for us to survive and move into our true human potential enabling us to lead a life worth living.

Looking at the psychology behind the ever increasing striving for enrichment of the few, the struggle for power and control, we can perceive a typical "reptilian brain" reaction of those feeling under threat, steeped in anxiety and fear of not being good enough; of being seen as weak or vulnerable with the fear of leaving themselves open to attack. They therefore act with a sense of entitlement, leaving the less fortunate, the poorer nations, the underdogs of society to be exploited even further; left to their own devices to struggle and muddle through life whilst others have more than enough.

Considering the situation from the angle of biology, we understand we are wired for survival; the need for this becomes clear if we imagine ourselves as cave people walking the earth, having to fight for our daily lives, provisions, food and water, surviving natural disasters purely on instinct, with a very rudimentary understanding of the world around.

The mind boggles, looking at our so called civilised world, that we might not have developed far beyond that and are still run by our reptilian brain reactions.

Despite all our knowledge, we seem to have entered yet another phase of upheaval, which we have seen many times repeated throughout history.

Have we learnt nothing from our past?

Part Two:

Unravelling past Patterns

Looking back at the great empires and civilisations throughout history, they all seem to have reached a plateau from which there was no going forward and, inevitably, they collapsed.

Over thousands of years since the beginning of modern humans (whose origin is still being debated to this day) wrongdoing has been inflicted on the poor, the weak the uneducated, the disadvantaged, downtrodden, the people who were thought to be inferior, worth less than the ruling classes, deemed too stupid to be able to understand the workings of the world.

Wars have been waged in the name of religion, exploring the world, producing and increasing boundless riches for some, and in their wake robbing peoples of their riches, their beliefs, their livelihood, their very lives, the very essence of their culture, robbing whole continents of their earthly riches and enslaving their population.

And yet, according to humanity's then level of consciousness, this is exactly what was deemed to be right, hence I feel we cannot judge this from our current own levels of awareness.

I strongly resonate with an idea I came across a couple of years ago, namely that mankind is developing in stages and, like a child, has undergone growth and consolidation phases. Apparently we are at teenage years now, which would explain the constant upheaval and uncertainty in our world.

With every new piece of learning and realisations about our existence, we grow that little bit more and are therefore capable of a greater awareness of who we really are and can then act accordingly.

In theory, humans' potential for development always existed, however, we lacked the capacity to understand and interpret the information around and within us.

Through the ages we reached various stages of mental, emotional and physical growth, leading to phases of levelling up. Our consciousness grows with every piece of learning, which in turn produces mental and emotional growth, facilitating a brain expansion so our consciousness changes. Unless inner growth has taken place alongside, we are unable to understand and draw the right conclusions, falling back into old, well established patterns of thinking. To put it bluntly, we are playing it safe.

To move onto a higher level, society has to break down and start again, until part of the brain has developed those collective neurones to instigate change from a new understanding of the world.

As an example to clarify:

For a minute, put your mind to children's behaviour.

How often do they seem wild and cruel to us when they poke and pull at a pet or hit out at a friend? Unless with great patience and care we teach them otherwise, and demonstrate with our own behaviour, they will not know any better.

Or think of a two year old who has not reached the developmental stage of being able to write spell or count, their brain is not ready yet as other things have to be learnt first, the brain has its own pace of developing those building blocks on which to base further learning.

41

Alongside the brain and biological development, there are also learnings in emotional growth, learning how to interact, love, care, and support each other.

Back to grown up society.

Our understanding of the world and the universe has been shaped in the past by philosophers, great thinkers and scientists in an effort to explain themselves, the world, the universe and our place within it.

Take Darwin or Newton, for example:

For centuries now, the old Newtonian and Darwinist views of humankind, and their scientific explanations have shaped our view of the world and how we act within it; however, with new scientific discoveries, the emergence of all things Quantum, and the resulting, relatively recent mind shifts, we have finally started to see things differently introducing us to new ideas and perspectives on all things living.

Isaac Newton (1642-1726) and his laws on physics, mathematics, and general science shaped the world of its days. Again, his thinking and subsequent conjectures were based on his own mind-brain and how far he had developed, drawing conclusions fitting the world's level of development at that time.

The same goes for Darwin (1809-1882) and his contributions to evolutionary biology. For his time he was a great mind, and in his writings, "On the origin of species", he talks about natural selection and the survival of the fittest which our whole society until very recently has been based on. This basic principle of evolution is, to this day, taught in schools around the world.

Only in the last twenty years have we come to understand and, therefore, able to contradict Darwin's explanations about our DNA and therefore how we act in the world.

The emergence of Epigenetics has proven that our DNA can be changed very fast by what we do, think and surround ourselves with. New brain science has found our brain will grow throughout our lifetime and is not, as formerly believed, unchangeable once we reach adulthood.

We have scientific proof now that we can control our thoughts. Neurones are firing with every word we speak, in our brain, in our heart, and what we speak and believe creates our inner and outer reality.

This newly gained knowledge gives us new windows on how the world functions. It puts us in control of ourselves; we are no longer victims of our DNA.

In short, Darwin's survival of the fittest does not cut it any longer.

Surprisingly enough, despite some of us having taken quantum leaps in our understanding of ourselves, our surroundings and how we see the world, not everyone is on board, the teachings in schools have not changed, young and adult minds alike are still being indoctrinated with learnings that no longer ring true.

We need a world whose paradigms are finally shifting faster than ever, in order for us to survive and move into our true human potential, enabling us to lead a life worth living.

There are some big questions we have to ask ourselves:

- How long before bigger changes will occur around the world?
- What is holding us back?

- Why are our mind, body and souls not filled with joy, creativity, harmony and healing?
- Why do we still live in a world full of anger, hatred, greed and feelings of not being good enough?

The truth is, I suspect, that our mind-body-emotion and spirit have not cleared out the "old stuff" which still permeates our system and our whole energy field, clinging to our DNA to be passed down to further generation.

What subconsciously are we holding onto?

I inevitably must ask myself how much of our very existence has been impacted by past trauma, now stuck in our reptilian brain, forcing reactions that are no longer relevant.

Trauma, defined as the impact of an event which has not been processed and hence has become stuck in our psyche, and in the recesses of our mind and the very cells of our body, producing a less than ideal blueprint for our thinking and how we behave during our lifetime, passing on past experiences via our genetic makeup, which is threatening the continuation of our existence.

To be able to move forward, we need to heal old wounds. Those wounds unwittingly inflicted on and by the human race, inflicted on each other and with it on ourselves, inflicted just the same on the earth as a whole organism.

I would like to remind you at this point that wars are still being waged, people are still fighting and killing each other on a daily basis, so it looks like we haven't learnt enough yet.

I ask again, why?

In search of answers, I would like to share some research on collective and generational unconscious trauma and its ability to pass along the memory of our DNA.

Research into past war / societal traumas:

Contrary to most people's belief that humans in the past were so used to fighting and constant striving for survival that they took wars and loss of life in their stride and carried on unaffected, new studies are emerging, showing a wholly different picture.

We have up to now not been able to collectively tune into that fact of past suffering because, for whatever, to my mind, protective reason, we thought that the past is the past and does not concern us.

However, as society has finally accepted that PTSD for example is not an imaginary hypochondriac's reaction to stress (yes that used to be the common consensus in the not too distant past) more research now shows that the warriors of past civilisations were quite familiar with various stress disorders.

For example, the writings of Geoffroi de Charny, a much celebrated knight of the 14th century, writes in his book about the life of a knight and the psychological consequences of having to kill people and fight for their own survival which resemble the symptoms of PTSD.

Taken from Science Nordic, violent knights feared post-traumatic stress, Kristian Sjorgen, translated by Michael de Laine.

Special response to combat trauma was found in Greek literature that could affect healing and mitigate psychological damage.

Socrates, a resilient and resourceful combat veteran, was keenly aware of the disabling stress and psychological damage of intense military service, and Plato was convinced that Greek tragedy and storytelling was going to counteract any traumatic experiences stemming from unprocessed traumatic war events.

Taken from The New Antiquity: Combat Trauma and the Ancient Greeks.

Peter Meineck, David Konstan, Combat Trauma and the Ancient Greeks. The New Antiquity. New York: Palgrave Macmillan, 2014. xiv, 310. ISBN 9781137398857

"The plague so ravaged the empire's professional armies that offensives were called off and abandoned farms and depopulated towns dotted the countryside from Egypt to Germany."

The psychological effects were, if anything, even more profound."

And from the writings of Aristides, we can glean the fear and then (the, their) survivor's guilt of those who did survive. This is taken from notes from the late 2nd century Roman Empire.

Smallpox again was a massive killer spreading through the roman empire and archaeologists working all over the old imperial territory still find amulets and little stones carved by people desperately trying to ward off the pestilence.

Taken from Smithsonian Magazine, Edward Watts.

The very existence of those written works and the fact that somebody made the effort of thinking and writing about it, proves to me that people then, like now, were struggling to understand the effects of wars on the soldiers themselves and the society collectively, and subsequently tried to find solutions.

For example, Plato is well known for using Greek Tragedy as a form of trauma therapy, which he believed could purge the individual and the society as a whole from the detrimental effects of wars.

Extremely interesting is the scientific research on how past trauma can be passed on to future generations.

Some of that research is in its infancy but would explain the phenomenon of trans generational trauma.

When scientists looked into DNA changes which occurred during those times of war and pandemics, they found no mutation to the DNA code itself (which would happen in inherited disease pattern) instead through the process of Epigenetics they found our body has the ability to tag messages, like leaving little post-it notes, onto the DNA structure which then in turn get passed on to future generations impacting people's stress response patterns over generations to come.

Info taken from Psych Central, Biological Psychiatry, PUBmed.

For example:

Studies into holocaust survivors found that second and third generation survivors showed a stronger stress response with more detrimental effects on their body, emotional and mental state than the first generation. Which I am inclined to think is because 2nd and 3rd generations are not aware of what they are carrying and therefore are unable to counteract the info which runs on an unconscious level, hence the person cannot take action to guard themselves against it.

Info taken from Bernd Steinbock, University of Western Ontario. bsteinbo@uwo.ca

Keywords: Stress, Intergenerational transmission, PTSD, placenta, sperm, Epigenetics

(PUBMed Central.

Parental advisory: maternal and paternal stress can impact offspring neurodevelopment

Jennifer C. Chan,1 Bridget M. Nugent,2 and Tracy L. Bale2

Author information Copyright and License information Disclaimer

Personal experience:

In my first year of CST (Cranial Sacral Therapy) training, attending a student group session with six therapists treating one person, we came across the following:

A young lady, let's call her S, in her twenties, came for treatment accompanied by her mother, who, with the permission of her daughter, wanted to sit in as an observer.

Reason for visit: obsessive fearful thoughts and dreams of not ever being able to become pregnant/nightmares of losing a baby.

During the treatment, a memory emerges of having lost a baby, which wasn't possible as the young lady had never been pregnant; once the extreme grief surfaced and released from her body, the mother opens up and shares this:

She herself had been pregnant, and lost the child, a few years before S. was born. She had been beside herself with grief and it had taken her many years to get over this; she had also feared she might never be able to become pregnant again but had never shared this with her daughter. The young lady's memory was actually that of her mother.

How could that be possible unless that deeply traumatic event had imprinted on the mother's DNA and was passed on to the daughter?

I have unravelled for you one part of the thread, of which I suspect there are many more, so how can we utilise those discoveries and the new science to take them forward into a new world?

Part three:

Spinning a new tale

By asking ourselves the simple question "What If" we are able to open a new narrative and we can start spinning a new tale.

What if?

- We see what we expect to see.
- We experience what we expect to experience.
- We believe what we have been taught to believe and are hence only able to perceive life from that angle.

To clarify, let me take you off on a tangent to consider an old narrative:

How did societies and different cultures perceive their gods in the past?

Angry gods, punishing gods who had to be appeased at all times, were really only reflections of our own primitive minds. The gods and heroes of ancient times were shaped from our own image, reflecting our own struggles and imbued with strengths we wished to possess; they were, at times spiteful, promiscuous, and violent.

In some cultures, the images were taken from nature, to explain the frightening and uncertain world around them, to explain natural disasters or just make sense of things nobody really understood.

Consider the ancient story of Adam and Eve: they were sinners, they had done wrong; they were punished by being banished from paradise and as a result we are all born with an original sin.

NB: When I first came across the idea of "the original sin" as a child, I was just as outraged as I was coming across the following paragraph:

"The sinister truth is that for communities to thrive, enemies are as necessary as friends. External danger binds the group together, reduces personal animosity, enhances mutual trust, promotes altruism and self-sacrifice. A society surrounded by enemies is unified and strong, a society without enemies divided and lax."

Taken from Archetypes, 1982 Dr Anthony Stevens.

To start the new narrative, I would like you to consider this:

- What if we looked at life from a different angle now, changed our viewpoint?
- What if the apple wasn't that of forbidden knowledge of good and evil?
- What if the original sin is actually ancient knowledge of past experiences, collective knowledge passed on via our DNA tags?

- What if we have been drip fed a lie based on very early experiences of our human existence, and the inevitable conclusions we have drawn were actually faulty?
- What if we have been indoctrinated with beliefs that life is dangerous, life has to be hard, life is fraught with stress, we have to conquer life? We have to become stronger, better, faster because if we don't we'll be unsuccessful, miserable and eventually dead?
- What if behind it all lies the fact of unprocessed events, tragedies, manmade and world disasters, traumatised people, a global mind as one, globally traumatised passing it on between us as unconsciously, we tune into and match each other's vibrational body, one trauma mind meets another and inevitably aligns in a self-perpetuating drama.

It seems clear to me that we need to go back, unravelling the threads into our past before we can move onto rewriting our story and spinning that new narrative.

The release of trans generational trauma which is still alive within us stirring up more anger hatred fear and anxiety, will free our energetic body and DNA from the past, leaving behind externalised knowledge which can no longer touch us and hence the learnings, the thoughts and ideas are there for us to perceive, observe and study, from a new level of consciousness.

Now, imagine a society which has accepted that we all carry from way back memory, scars, and triggers, passed down the generations and living with them whilst unawares that we do.

Imagine replacing the old trauma and the attached unconscious reactions with love, curiosity, kindness, understanding and acceptance of self and others, seeing life through the lens of empathy, the knowledge and final understanding that we can be bound together by a new narrative.

Imagine a new conscious world where everyone is allowed and supported in living to their best potential fulfilling their soul purpose, allowed to learn and grow in the knowledge that they are supported along the way, feeling safe in the knowledge that they are allowed to live on this earth as custodians and part of a bigger universal reality and consciousness.

Imagine…

We have come to understand and accept that we are at all times connected to everything around us, that our surrounds are a reflection of our innermost self, we are nature and nature is us; we are the universe and the universal force is within us.

Now imagine:

Whatever we think, do, imagine, we create; our surroundings are a reflection of ourselves and instead of creating chaos, anger, hatred and despair we are free to create a life on Earth in the knowledge that Eve picking the apple did not cast them out into the wilderness of life, but instead gave them the enlightenment to create their own heaven on earth.

Are you ready to collectively start spinning a new thread, one which will lead us all into a New Paradigm way of life, thus creating a better world for all of us?

Wouldn't that be a better way for all of us?

Note by the lead author

As someone with an interest in the concept of generational trauma and the idea that our DNA can be manipulated (for better, or worse) I find Andrea's chapter utterly fascinating.

Using her own knowledge and drawing on examples from the past, she shows us how the world we live in today has been shaped by those who came before us. How past wars, natural disasters, plagues etc. deeply affected our ancestors and filtered down the generations to affect us negatively in the here and now.

Andrea explains how modern humans are still "wired for survival". But survival in the 21st century is very different to surviving in the time of our hunter gatherer antecedents. We no longer have to protect ourselves from the dangers of predatory animals as we go about our day to day business, but our brains are still wired as if we were and the fight/flight response still kicks in.

That road rage you experience when confronted by what you perceive as a dangerous driver will cause the same chemical reaction in your brain as your Paleolithic ancestor experienced when attacked by a wolf. Unfortunately. we come across incidents on a daily basis in our modern lives which cause the spike in the stress hormones cortisol and adrenaline (the fight/flight response). Whereas I doubt very much that our ancestors experienced traumatic events on such an incessant basis.

Our ancient forbears did experience the fight/flight reflex – just not every day, multiple times per day, so their bodies were able to return to a normal calm state – unlike their modern day descendants who live in a constant stress state.

Andrea asks us to imagine a world where we have learned to fully expunge the trauma of the past and live to the best of our individual potential whilst knowing and accepting that we are all part of a vast Universal collective.

I, for one, can get onboard with this.

How about you?

Chapter 4

From Fear to Curiosity, Wonder and Love - A Foot in Two Worlds

by Beverly Radley

Introduction

"Embracing the New Paradigm - From Fear to Curiosity, Wonder and Love" is a chapter that delves into the profound journey of transitioning from a fear-based existence to one rooted in love and harmony. In a world filled with turmoil and division, this transition becomes all the more compelling. To explore the challenges and steps required to make this shift, from letting go of old foundations built on fear to understanding and reclaiming one's authentic self.

At the crossroads of change, it feels like one foot is firmly rooted in the old world, while the other yearns to step into the new. The fear of the unknown can be paralysing, but to embrace the new, one must first release the old and dissolve the foundations of fear that have held society captive for too long. Moving from a duality world to one of unity.

Listening to oneself, connecting with the Earth, and adopting the African concept of "Ubuntu" or "I am because you are" (we'll talk more about this later) are essential elements of this transformation. It also needs to involve reimagining education and community and finding the balance between light and darkness.

This chapter serves as a guide for those who seek a new world, a new way of being, and the path to living from a place of love instead of lack. It emphasises the importance of collaboration over competition and the realisation that individual well-being is intertwined with the well-being of others. Ultimately, it encourages you to embark on the journey from fear to love, recognising that it's a path worth taking for a world guided by harmony, peace, and love and it starts with ourselves.

From Fear to Love,

The transition from a fear-based existence to one rooted in love and harmony is a personal journey and a collective one. It is a voyage that demands a leap of faith, trust in the unknown, and the release of the grip of fear that has held humanity hostage for far too long. As the ancient Japanese art of Jin Shin Jyutsu states, "be the unknowing!"

Letting go of the old, creating space, allowing and breathing. Getting curious and allowing the child-like wonder to reemerge. This creates space for the new energies to flow. To let the new in, the past must be allowed to rest and be released. The divine feminine way of receiving as opposed to the masculine energy of forcing or pushing. Divine feminine energy is present in both males and females alike, its receptive energy. Old habits and conditionings of people pleasing, and being nice for recognition and acknowledgement, must fall away, leaving way for being kind not only to ourselves, with self-compassion and self-care because "we cannot give from an empty cup".

As we give to ourselves, we have more to share and give to others, not from a place of resentment, but from a place of love. Living in the new paradigm for me is about living in the present.

Calling all parts back from all dimensions and encircling my energy in a net of love to hold me present, feeling safe, secure and grounded in this magical present moment.

"The present is a gift."

It can be perceived as hard to let go of things when you don't know what's coming. Take the time to allow the old list of things that are based on fear, surrounded by lack, doubt and disbelief to dissolve. Anything built on fear foundations is not going to be sustainable. It needs to be built on a foundation of love. Much of this fear can be inherited beliefs and habits that, with awareness, we can change. To do that, we have to take down the old… that feels like it might take effort.

"Awareness is key."

However, when we trust and we do not cling to it, all that is not needed falls away naturally if! Pause for a moment and feel; is there tension in your jaw, your neck and shoulders? Are you habitually holding on? Or in the brace position wanting to keep control of everything? How is that working for you?

Sometimes there is an acknowledgement of sadness and, most definitely, a different way of thinking is needed.

How can that be achieved?

The self-belief that there is something better that we can build, or allow something to be involved in a future based on love and joy, rather than fear and lack and desperation.

That feeling of holding tight to the hosepipe, wondering where the flow went. When we let go, things flow!

Fear is a tightening of the grip of a lack of belief in one's self and life.

Taking the time to ease into how we feel, to know whether these feelings and emotions are ours, which we have carried with us for many years, or ones we've picked up from others. Or even an awareness of where this energy came from, perhaps collected from others during the day.

Ground and release this energy and take a moment to allow the Earth to absorb all that we no longer need and to share with us her infinite wisdom of millennia.

Each day starting with grounding in the present moment again.

Connection to Earth

In the pursuit of a world based on love and harmony, connecting with the Earth is essential. Just as old emotions and beliefs are let go of the Earth is allowed to absorb all that is no longer needed. In return, the Earth shares her infinite wisdom. Taking a moment to listen, find stillness and breathe in love while breathing out gratitude is vital for grounding in the new paradigm.

Try this simple breathing and use this simple meditation:

Centre yourself and feel your little toes on the floor. Spread out all your toes and feel your heels resting on the ground.

Take a breath in and feel the airflow over your lip.

Listen and find stillness,

Breathe out…

Breathe in love…

Breathe out gratitude …

Breathe in love …

Breathe out gratitude.

Congratulations - you have started your journey to being and sharing more love.

Emotions - Hate and Anger

The hate and anger that is perpetuated based on lack, greed and fear is what we need to let go of, but fear can make us hold on even more. When we are full of these emotions, we become saturated, frozen, stuck, and un-resourceful. No capacity for thought or time to consider our reactions. We react instead of responding.

"When our body is full of emotion, and our head is a pressure cooker. How can we give and receive love?"

Personally, I have found regulating my parasympathetic nervous system with somatic support helpful to take me out of the fight, flight, freeze and fawn and the dysregulation that happens.

The Crossroads of Change

We embark on a journey exploring the profound transition from the crumbling old paradigm to the dawn of a new reality. Fear, born from the dissolution of the familiar, tightly bonds our attachment to outdated ways.

Our emotions, intricately entwined with our thoughts, can become unconsciously addictive, weaving threads of fear, betrayal and envy into the fabric of our existence.

As we navigate the crossroads of change, one foot hesitates in the security of the old world while the other yearns to step boldly into the new. The challenge lies in releasing the familiar old comfort blanket, even when fear is present, marking the daunting nature of the transition.

In my office is a Buddhist quote:

"In the end, all that matters is …

How well did I live?

How well did I love?

How well did I learn to let go?"

In my experience, learning to "love" has been a more accessible journey compared to the profound challenge of "letting go!". The true wisdom, I have discovered, emerges when we are compelled to release something incredibly precious. A situation where "letting go" is not a choice, but a change thrust upon you. This process unfolds as a poignant lesson in life's intricate tapestry. Traversing the journey of grief and loss and all its intricate twists and turns, solitude and devastation and heartache as well as glimmers of the remembrance of joyful memories.

From experience, many of the things I've had to let go of, I didn't get a choice and I have had to let go of so many things and people that were so precious. It has changed my world, my view of the world and what I want and need.

What is truly important?

Dissolving the Foundations of Fear

The initial step on this transformative journey involves knowledge, the very foundations upon which life is constructed. Many of these foundations are rooted in fear; fear of scarcity, loss, and the unknown; that hinder the creation of a new world. It's crucial to construct a base founded on love, dismantling the structures of fear that have held society captive for too long.

When we don't receive, fear of lack sets in, forgetting that the world is abundant, echoing nature's inherent abundance without the concept of fear or lack. While there are fluctuations in what we have, sometimes more, sometimes just what we need, it's essential to acknowledge that your present situation is perfect and complete. Being present with it allows for a holistic understanding, and from there, decisions about necessary actions can be made. If change is desired, it's possible, but it begins with "accepting what is".

The perpetual struggle to resist acceptance consumes energy and becomes exhausting. Release this wasted energy, redirecting it toward purposeful action. Curiosity and wonder. Movement and emotion are equal to energy, and channelling this energy wisely allows for a transformative shift.

Emotion = Energy + Motion

Listening to the Self

In the pursuit of embracing the new paradigm, attentive self-listening becomes pivotal. Distinguishing between authentic emotions and beliefs, versus those imposed by society or absorbed from others, demands introspection and self-awareness; a process of understanding one's inner landscape and reclaiming the authentic self.

61

This authenticity serves as a compass, steering away from confusion and guiding choices rooted in love rather than gluttony, greed, and excess.

Recognising there are ample resources, but their distribution is unequal, calls for a collapse of power struggles. The concept of "Ubuntu" from an African tradition illustrates interconnectedness – "I am because you are".

"I am because you are." A very real example of this is a group of children who were given a bucket of apples and told whoever ran to the bucket first would win it all. The group of children joined hands and ran to the bucket together. When asked, they said, "why would one person be happy with all the apples when the others have nothing?".

This ethos fosters a collective approach, as exemplified by children sharing apples, reflecting the essence of Ubuntu. Transitioning to the new paradigm involves adopting the idea of Ubuntu, emphasising that individual well-being is intricately tied to the well-being of others. It's a shift from seeking happiness solely for oneself to striving for contentment and joy for all. This shift is a vital aspect of embracing the new paradigm, rooted in love rather than lack.

To navigate the transition, trust becomes essential. Determining what needs to be let go and what to receive requires overcoming the fear of the unknown. Despite the challenges, choosing to live in love and peace is a conscious decision. The lyrics of Sam Garrett's song, "I choose to live in love" serves as my inspiration daily, to centre myself in my heart, resonating with the desire to find a new world and way of being, despite the fear and ego that may arise. Personal experiences of letting go, even when not by choice, have reshaped perspectives on what truly matters to me in the world.

—

Letting go of numerous things and people has been a transformative journey. In this process, I've discovered that material possessions don't hold the significance I once thought. This shedding of attachments has profoundly shaped my world, altering my perspective on what truly matters and what I genuinely want and need in life.

Shifting from Fear to Love

The most significant challenge on this journey is releasing the fear that keeps the old world anchored. Fear of scarcity, greed, and the unknown are powerful forces. It makes us hold on to the old even when it no longer serves. This fear blinds us to the abundance of resources in the world and perpetuates power struggles that have caused much suffering.

I want to look at my understanding of riches and of wealth. My change in the need for stuff, realising that all those belongings were to fill a hole generated by a feeling of lack and desperately trying to fill that empty feeling.

I have a heart filled with love. Some of that love cannot be given to where I wanted to give it, so I now need to find a different way to share that love.

That is my way of stepping into this new world, having a new world when my heart is open and I'm able to share the love that I have for myself and for others in a beautiful way, in a loving way, in a way that doesn't cause harm to others.

Reimagining Education and Community

School - based on curiosity, creativity and love of learning in your way.

In the new world, education is based on curiosity, creativity, and a love of learning. Collaboration takes precedence over competition, and communities prioritise sustainability. Honouring ancestors, traditions, and the wisdom of nature is at the forefront. Listening to nature's whispers and appreciating the beauty and abundance of the natural world is vital.

Embracing the Balance

Ultimately, the transition to the new paradigm is about finding balance. Embracing both the light and the darkness is necessary. The darkness is not to be feared, but accepted and understood. It holds its own gifts and wisdom. Both light and dark are required to create harmony.

Stepping into this new world, carrying love, belief, and dreams, is essential. Recognising that one is a human being, not a human "doing" is a key aspect of the journey. In the connection to nature, the true self is found.

The journey from fear to love is not easy, but it is a journey worth taking. It is a path to a world where harmony, peace, and love are the guiding principles. In this new paradigm, the transformation sought, both individually and collectively, can be achieved.

In this new paradigm, the transformation we seek, both individually and collectively, is not just a dream; it's an achievable reality. Together, we can build a world where love prevails and we leave fear behind.

Are you ready to let go of the old, embrace the new, and journey from fear to love to create a world of harmony and peace?

Below is a channelled message from purple viola; when I listen to the whispers of nature, poetry comes through. I thought I would share nature's wisdom as gifted to me by purple viola to see what you feel. Next time you are in nature, have a listen, the new paradigm is waiting for you to hear its whispers, it's ready to help you see the way forward and take the next step.

Purple viola. Made in my garden Sheffield 23rd June 2021.

From the darkness, there is the tiniest speck of light.

Deep in the despair of what you are feeling, there is the tiniest bit of hope.

Something to hold onto; a snippet of light.

Be in the shadow, allow the darkness, don't be afraid of it. In the darkness, if you allow it, there is growth.

When you fight it, there is fear,

When you allow it, there is comfort in the surrendering. The acceptance that light is needed as much as darkness. The two align and make harmony.

It is our fear that holds us hostage! What is it you are afraid of?

Acceptance and understanding of the darkness is what is needed, not fear and judgement.

Allow it to settle with you like a wise old friend. Being kind to you, as though you have known each other for years.

Welcome the darkness and see what gifts it has to share.

The energy to keep it at bay is exhausting and continuous.

The fear is driving the ship! But if you allow it, the ship will float with the waves and not fight against them.

Rest for a while within the darkness; give it room, give it space, give it time and your attention.

Then its power through fear will be released.

Stop and look at it, stop running, be stilled and then its power is released.

(my dog Rosco returned to be by the essence bowl)

Let the light tonight be the gift in your heart, a way forward to acknowledge the light but not be overwhelmed by it.

To give it space, but not let it be the only thing in your life.

Welcome in the balance and harmony between light and dark.

Love, believe, dream.

And step out into this new world.

Note by the lead author

Shortly after I first approached her to take part in this book, Beverly experienced a personal tragedy that shook her world to the very core. I am more grateful than I can say that, despite everything that was going on for her, she decided she was still able to contribute her wonderful chapter.

Beverly has written about the necessity of humanity moving "from fear to love" – sounds like a simple statement, doesn't it? But, as we are all too aware, often the simplest things are the hardest to achieve – particularly when it involves having to address emotions!

Her chapter focuses on love and collaboration and she pays particular attention to the African concept of "Ubuntu" – "I am because you are."

I'd heard of Ubuntu before (not least because it is also the name given to a Linux operating system!) but I decided to look up a definition and came across the following from the African Journal of Social Work dated 2020:

A collection of values and practices that people of Africa or of African origin view as making people authentic human beings. While the nuances of these values and practices vary across different ethnic groups, they all point to one thing – an authentic individual human being is part of a larger and more significant relational, communal, societal, environmental and spiritual world.

Look at the last bit… *an authentic individual human being is part of a larger and more significant relational, communal, societal, environmental and spiritual world…*it makes a lot of sense doesn't it?

Beverly also talks about letting go of the past and instead choosing to live in the present, which mirrors Andrea Hochgatterer's idea that we need to let go of generational trauma. I love that each of them has touched upon the same issue…almost as if it were meant to be!

I'll end with this wonderful quote:

"When we don't receive, fear of lack sets in, forgetting that the world is abundant, echoing nature's inherent abundance without the concept of fear or lack."

Chapter 5

The Time for Change is NOW

by Elke Wallace

Introduction - The importance of focusing on the solution

The world is at a crossroads. It has come to a point where things can go horribly wrong for the whole planet, humans, flora and fauna alike, if people won't wake up and unite, both on a global scale but also locally, to stop this intensifying attack on our freedom and relentless power grab and sort out the mess the world is currently in.

Governments that are not worth the word, self-servingly filling their pockets and bank accounts and determined to be the puppets of over-arching global organisations that are out for a complete power grab and the restriction of all freedoms for average citizens.

Countless books have been written questioning, researching, investigating what is going on and diving deep into all the problems we face. What I have not seen much of are books that focus more on the solutions rather than dwelling on the issues. And this is why I have decided to contribute to this book.

Reclaiming Personal Power and Taking Personal Responsibility

We are living in a world that constantly bombards us with information in a nanny-state fashion - what we can, cannot, should or should not do. We are discouraged from a deep connection with nature, starting, as one example, with persuading us not to eat certain foods that serve our health and wellbeing. Seeds of confusion and division are planted in people and hyped up in mainstream channels.

In fact, this has been going on for centuries or even millennia and longer, but with modern means of communication, it feels much more intense and can lead to overwhelm.

But there is ancient wisdom from different corners of the world, for example, from India and Hawaii, that teaches us how everything is connected and alive, how we can utilise nature for our benefit while caring for it, and how we can draw on eternal energy to reclaim our inner power to live fulfilled lives, away from distractions and attempts to divide and control humanity.

Those teachings include taking personal responsibility for all our choices, actions and behaviours and learning to control our thoughts and emotions to thrive and be in tune with nature and its rhythms, cycles and energy. However, the teachings also make us aware that all our choices, actions, behaviours and even thoughts can affect everyone and everything around us and everywhere.

These teachings are timeless ancient wisdom and rules for living in a more harmonious and interconnected way that still apply today, no matter how much the powers that be are trying to divert us away from them to become slaves in their matrix.

To create a better world, it is necessary to return to the ancient wisdom, rules and teachings and apply them to our daily lives. They form the foundation of a change for the better.

Life Skills Education – Nature, money, nutrition, body and mind

The modern education system was created in the first place to create a literate workforce that could read, write and have some mathematical and science skills.

It is an education system that has more and more become a system of conditioning children and young people into new alien and ideological concepts thought out by post-war academics with curricula determined by those in national and international top institutions and authorities. Very often, teachers and lecturers are trained to teach but don't have a full understanding of the subject and only teach based on textbook knowledge.

It is an education system that discourages creativity and playfulness and finds if more important to confuse children and young people about gender and identity rather than teaching them real life skills about entrepreneurship, money and personal finance, how to grow fruit and vegetables, nutrition and how body, brain and mind work.

It is an education system based on a one-for-all model that rewards those who have the mental capabilities to follow curricula but easily leaves those with neurodivergent conditions and disabilities behind (unless they get into a special school, which is not a great idea either as they are not socially inclusive). Everyone's brain is different.

Every person has different preferences to process information and different talents, but talents often get overlooked or suppressed.

—

It is time to bring the education system into the 21st century!

- Educational institutions need to be transparent in where they get funding from to avoid being influenced by any global agendas or ideologies (something that happened and possibly still happens in the medical field).

- Life Skills like entrepreneurship, money and personal finance, how to grow fruit and vegetables, healthy nutrition and how body, brain and mind work need to be integrated into all curricula to prepare our children and young people for life.

- We need teachers and lecturers with sound knowledge and a background in the subject they are teaching.

- Creativity deserves to be encouraged and fostered, as it is the foundation of innovation.

- Education needs to be more flexible and more tailored to the needs and talents of individuals.

- Curricula should be independent of global agendas and ideologies, based on human and environmental needs as well as the science and knowledge of nature and its laws.

What should not be forgotten and should be included in the revamp of the education system, is to ensure children and young people are taught healthy social and communication skills as well as instilling a sense of responsibility for their actions and the consequences such actions can have on their immediate environment. This will also contribute to prepare them for life after the education system and for becoming responsible citizens and human beings.

A Holistic Health Approach – Prevention, solutions and cures

Our health is our biggest wealth and we are creatures of nature, connected to nature, each one unique in genetics, metabolism, physical and mental function.

The over-digitalisation, environmental pollution (that includes chemicals in personal care items and food), overload of synthetically created pharmaceutical drugs and the increased disapproval of natural health remedies by the pharmaceutical industry and their influence on health care policies and training of medical staff, has led to a disconnect from nature.

Different cultures have created different systems of health care, prevention and cure, often based on ancient knowledge from people who had a much closer connection to nature than we currently do.

We are often told in mainstream sources that certain illnesses or diseases cannot be "cured" (and alternative healthcare approaches are not even allowed to use that word without the likelihood of being sued by some pharma-related body), but there are alternative approaches to healthcare and health prevention available.

Some of these approaches are based on ancient knowledge, like Ayurveda from India or Chinese Medicine and Acupuncture, or Shamen or Medicine People from other native indigenous peoples on the planet.

To provide a more tailored healthcare system based on people's genetic makeup, metabolism, etc. all approaches to health care deserve EQUAL recognition, funding, promotion and the right to be applied.

Pharma is first and foremost a business focused on making profits for its investors, which are very often people in politics and philanthropy interested primarily in earning a big reward on their investments. If you are reading this with disbelief, I highly encourage you to research the history and development of our current Western medical system, starting with the names of Andrew Carnegie and John Rockefeller in the late 1800s in the U.S.

To achieve a more equal playing field in health care, I have the following ideas that may be more like a David vs. Goliath fight but are necessary to reduce the advantage and power of big pharma:

- A high percentage of pharma profits have to be diverted into local communities and healthcare facilities - WITHOUT asking medical staff to be their "sales force" as in prescribing only pharmaceuticals.

- The medical system (including psychiatry) must be changed in the way all nurses, doctors and other medical staff are trained in nutrition and the effects of chemical substances in food on body and mind, as well as alternative approaches to

74

someone's health issues, so they can refer patients to alternative healthcare solutions if those were more suitable for the patient's needs.

- More training provisions and opportunities for alternative healthcare practitioners.

- Public education campaigns to promote alternative healthcare approaches and their validity, as many studies are conducted, which are currently mostly being kept out of the public domain.

- All healthcare approaches get equal opportunities for funding, promotion of services and public exposure to make people aware to end the overarching power of the pharma industry.

A holistic incorporation of all available approaches to healthcare could offer more choices and better outcomes for everyone.

Real democracy - Reshaping politics and leadership

Let's start again with what the actual definition of democracy is. According to the Oxford Languages definition, democracy is "a system of government by the whole population or all the eligible members of a state, typically through elected representatives." Well, yes, it typically is but the real meaning of democracy as per the Council of Europe makes it a bit clearer as it goes into the roots of the word. "The word democracy comes from the Greek words *demos*, meaning people, and *kratos* meaning power"; so democracy can be thought of as "power of the people": a way of governing which depends on the will of the people.

As things stand right now, there is not really much "power of the people", because the only power we people have is to vote representatives into a parliament based on what they promise they would do for the benefit of the public (at least that's how most people vote), which such representative quickly forget once they have been voted in as members or a parliament (and even quicker if they get into government). There are rare occasions where a referendum can be called, but that is still not enough "power for the people".

As the current system is full of corruption, with governments more often acting in accordance with the instructions of lobbyists and leaders of unelected higher institutions or corporations, the whole system of governance and politics needs a complete overhaul to be fit to serve the public. Some ideas could be:

- We need the end of "career politicians", of people who go into politics following university studies only and without ever having held positions of employment or experience of entrepreneurship and running a business.

- Anyone who wants to get into parliament should have worked in a field of employment for at least 5 – 10 years.

- Government ministers should come from leadership positions in their field, again having worked in their field for at least 5-10 years. What use is a Minister of Economics who has never run a business, a Minister for Education, who never been Head Teacher in a big school, or a Minister for Health, who has never worked in, or run a hospital, to give a few examples.

- What I am sure of, is that politicians and leaders in positions of public office need to be fully transparent about their income and expenses (including all investments) with rules in place that they will not be allowed to undertake other consultancy work or hold positions as board members or similar on big corporations or organisations.

- They also need to be accountable to the public with the possibility of getting sacked without a Golden Handshake if they are not efficient in their work or break rules re transparency or links to big organisations.

The difficult thing is how to find suitable leaders and select them for election (if they don't put themselves forward). There is a possibility that leaders of their relevant field could get together to select suitable candidates for parliament, vetted by some independent people before approval. This is only a suggestion, as I'm not sure about the best solution.

Changing the political and leadership system in that way could be a allow more "people power" and a more realistic democracy than we have right now.

Real Environmentalism – Preserving and caring for flora and fauna

Nature is our source of food, source of healing, place of recreation – and if we do not treat it with the respect and care it deserves, we will pay the price.

The increase of health problems in people and a diversification of our food away from natural sources, plus the effects of chemicals in food production, is already an indicator of that.

While we are getting bombarded with Net Zero claims and fear stories, I do not see enough publicity about plastic polluting oceans and coastlines, illegal waste or sludge dumping on large scales, corporations polluting water, land and air, how farmers are encouraged to give up farming (remember: farming is vital for our food supply) and how the often sacred land of native and indigenous peoples are being coercively taken over or bought for pennies for the sake of progress, building of pipelines or other industrial plants.

The idea of renewable energy is great, but even solar panels require hazardous chemicals for their operation (which, when leaked, can destroy furniture and other materials – this happened to my sister years ago with their insurance reluctant to pay out), and wind turbines also require oil as lubricant, 80 gallons per turbine which must be changed once a year. Plus, neither solar panels and wind turbines are easily recycled due to their components.

Suggestions to avoid further environmental destruction, the preservation of nature and our food supply, to respect rights and sacred lands of indigenous peoples and to give all living creatures a chance to survive could include:

- Policies to penalise and even shut down the operations of big polluters and redistribute their assets to clean up environmental damage they caused or are causing, all with proper enforcement and without opportunities or loopholes to wriggle out of their obligations.

- Publicly funded scientific research into how best to deal with any plastics waste, decommissioning industrial plants including wind turbines and solar panels, and finding alternatives that cause less harm to the environment.

- Ensure the continuation of organic agriculture and farming without harmful pesticides and fertilisers and use natural means of crop protection and while offering a healthy environment for all farm animals.

- Reward people for caring for the environment, taking part in clean-ups, growing own food supplies, nature and animal conservation, etc.

- Proper protection of rights of indigenous native peoples to their lands and asking them in a respectful way to help us with their knowledge of nature and how to best care for it.

Only reverting to nature and its laws can help us to create a healthier environment and a world where all living creatures and living things can thrive.

Creating Peace – Dismantling the War Machine

One would think we have learned from the two major World Wars of the 20th Century that it would be more beneficial to seek other solutions to disagreements between nations than fighting each other while destroying the environment, towns, cities and villages and killing countless innocent lives. But no! Local wars are still being fought. Remember Yemen, Israel/Palestine and Ukraine as some recent and examples.

This has to end – NOW! It is time to STOP!

It's time to replace fighting and warfare with communication and negotiation, time to put differences aside for the sake of humanity, time for acceptance and tolerance of each other, and finding ways of cooperation and collaboration. It's time to stop wasting more human lives in pursuit of power and control – and especially to stop the seemingly endless profiteering of the war machine and weapons industry. They and their investors (which most certainly include members of governments and other authorities or institutions) play a key role in why wars are perpetuated.

To create peace and a better world, I suggest the following:

- Dissolving and dismantling the war machine and all weapons manufacturers.

- Redistribution of one part of their financial assets

    o to care for the maimed and injured,

    o to rebuild living spaces and infrastructure and

    o to decontaminate and clean up the environment.

- Redistribution of another part of financial assets and investments to improve local health care provisions, education and other local infrastructure projects.

- Weapons manufacturing plants are to be dismantled, resources diverted into other industries, and any environment damaged by weapons production has to be decontaminated and restored.

It is time to create lasting peace once and for all.

Reorganisation of the Financial System – Transparency and fairer redistribution

I have more recently come to learn about and understand the mindset of the wealthy, i.e. they make money to invest it to make even more. That isn't necessarily a bad thing, but it stops being good when wealth creation turns some people into greedy, power-hungry and control crazy psychopaths. Money and wealth are not the bad thing, but money and wealth in the wrong hands is.

Money hoarded and stored away is no use, it needs to fluctuate and move quickly. It is a tool to attribute perceived value to goods, services, anything that value can be attached to or perceived of.

What needs to change are the distribution and re-allocation of funds collected by government by means of taxation, as well as a meaningful distribution of profits made by big corporations. Along with the introduction of rounded financial education from childhood and the encouragement of entrepreneurship to offer equal opportunities for everyone.

Some ideas to change to a fairer distribution of financial wealth and re-investment in communities and local areas rather than big corporations and their shares could be:

- Simplification of the tax system and a transparent distribution of tax money WITHIN local areas and the country FIRST before allocating any finances for abroad.

- A high percentage of the profits of large corporations could be allocated to environmental preservation, healthcare-related projects and education and/or urgent needs or local areas.

- Businesses and corporations to be encouraged to invest inland instead of relocating production to cheaper countries.

- Lobbying of politicians and donations to political parties to be outlawed.

- Corruption to be outlawed and with heavy fines and other penalties.

- Finding ways to stop companies and individuals putting their wealth in tax havens abroad.

The basis for such ideas is, of course, is a complete overhaul of the political system, as discussed above.

Decentralisation – Why Globalisation is not the Answer

The Internet, emails, mobile phones and digitalisation have brought the world much closer together. We can easily communicate with people on the other side of the planet, buy and sell to and from other countries and travel has become much easier thanks to more automated processes. Ease and speed provide convenience – but that does not apply to every area of life.

While I appreciate the closer global connectedness of people and opportunities for businesses, the more globalised landscape has seen a drive towards monopolisation or large-scale companies that has driven many small businesses out; either because businesses could not compete with the larger competitors or because the larger firms gobbled up smaller firms and integrated them into their structure at the cost of a local presence, and with the loss of jobs.

It's time to turn the tide, stop further centralisation and monopolisation of authoritarian powers, corporations and organisations; it's time for decentralisation, which is defined by Oxford Languages as "the transfer of control of an activity or organisation to several local offices or authorities rather than one single one."

Centralisation itself is like applying a "one way for all" approach, which never works. Every person is different. Every local area, region, country is different. Every culture is different. And they all deserve respect and attention by assessing and offering means and opportunities most needed by people in local areas, regions, countries, which cannot be achieved by centralisation.

- Decentralisation could mean local areas governing themselves with more autonomy to make their own decisions that are more suitable to their environment and circumstances.

- Decentralisation allows for more choices, opportunities and a variety of information from different sources that may all be relevant. Let's remember, there is never just one side to a story.

- Decentralisation and breaking up large corporations could bring more opportunities into local areas for jobs and the creation of small and medium-sized businesses and entrepreneurship.

Decentralisation is the way forward with better opportunities for everyone.

Closing Thought

There is a lot to do to create a happier and healthier world that serves humans, nature and its living beings with the care and respect everyone and everything deserves.

A foundation for this is to unite people of all backgrounds, faiths, cultures with open hearts and minds with the willingness, wisdom and knowledge to draw up eternal energy to create the necessary changes on a global level.

Let's create collaboration instead of competition and unity instead of division, all based on unconditional love and acceptance.

Note by the lead author

Elke has chosen to take a very pragmatic and problem solving approach to the question of what a new paradigm world would look like.

Covering everything from the world's monetary situation to how best to educate our children and stop the incessant wars, she has examined why we are in the current mess and how we can change things – for the better.

What I found particularly interesting is that although on the face of it her chapter is very solution focused, if you read a little more closely, you will find that she talks about connectedness and love throughout. Connecting to nature. Connecting with each other. Collaboration over competition. Sharing. Redistribution of wealth. Respect for each other and the world.

Central to her thought process is decentralisation – which may, on the face of it, seem to contradict the mantra of connection – it doesn't, if you examine what she means by decentralisation.

What Elke (and I) would like to see is individuals, nation states, cities, towns, villages being allowed to be themselves with their own beliefs and ways of doing things instead of trying to compel everyone to become a homogenised mass of humanity. This, of course, comes with the proviso that in doing so, no harm is done to others. Decentralising does not give people the carte balance to be push their ideology (whatever it may be) onto others!

This is the quote that landed most firmly with me: "A foundation for this is to unite people of all backgrounds, faiths, cultures with open hearts and minds with the willingness, wisdom and knowledge to draw up eternal energy to create the necessary changes on a global level."

Chapter 6

Leading With Love

by Femke Williams

Nobody can tell you how to live your life. There is no readily available answer. There are only suggestions. Possible solutions. Philosophical guidance. Religions that pour their answers into dogmas and absolutes.

Nobody is perfect. Although actually, we are all perfect in our own rights. But then again, who decides what is 'perfect' anyway?

Living With Chaos

We are all on different levels of personal growth, and so it is not up to us to tell another how to live their life. So many of us have suffered relational trauma from a very young age, which can show up as a lot of very painful unhealthy patterns in our present or future relationships, growing up and into (young) adulthood. As I see it, this is significantly contributing to the main reasons why there is so much anger, sadness and frustration going round within our society at present, and it is now coming to a climax. People are ready to explode because of 'the way of the world' and there being 'so many idiots' who don't think like they do.

It causes hate, resentment and jealousy; and I suppose it's much easier to just blame everything and everyone else for the shortcomings in our life and in the world, and to ignore looking within as to how we can gain control over our own emotions and how to positively change and impact our personal circumstances, our patterns of behaviour and our health.

In our fast-paced 21st century world, our society is carrying more grief, unprocessed trauma and physical health problems than even 10 years ago. On top of inherited ancestral patterns and unresolved issues through the generations in the past 100 years or so (premature deaths, famine, war etc.), things have changed and evolved incredibly rapidly. Some for the better (i.e. around medicine and longevity), but overall there is a high level of control with respect to how we can 'be', work and what we can have. There isn't really any room for slowing down, relaxation, de-stressing, healing, following passions, or true connection. Significant global and interpersonal events have highlighted the vulnerabilities in our inner and outer world; we are living with chaos.

As a health and wellbeing and energy worker, I care about the natural world, wildlife and people, and I have a deep calling to be a positive change agent in the world. I recognise that some of the philosophies, approaches and systems are outdated, based on outdated beliefs and control, and how we are now more and more seeking holistic approaches and sustainable solutions which are going to lead to long-term healing and resolution. I want to do this for myself, my family, my clients, my direct environment and ultimately the World.

I want to share my wisdom, gifts and lived experience with others – like I know so many way-seekers are looking to do too.

I'd like to add to people's toolkit for looking after their physical and emotional health and wellbeing with a variety of evidence-based approaches and effective strategies; techniques that integrate the revered wisdom of the past with the innovative approaches of today. It is possible to bridge the gap between Eastern and Western medicine (as we do need the best of both worlds), and we can also tap into the wisdom of plant medicine (nutrition) and the Northern and Southern Hemisphere, like the seasons, life cycles and universal wellness.

Becoming Who We Are

We are all looking to stabilise ourselves – to expand our capacity, and to become whole and unlock our true potential. To me, it is essential that each and every one of us individually tends to our own healing, so that we can go from our wounded places and traumas to 'harvest' the gold and wisdom from our learnings and to pay these forward. We all have so much to give! We just need to remember what it is we came here to do.

So how do we go about doing that? For one, we can start to become more aware of what is actually going on for us, specifically in 8 key areas of our life; relationships, environment, nutritional health, emotional health, movement, lifestyle and pace, financial health, and Life Purpose – which is directly linked to spirituality. All of these key areas need to be brought into the light, aligned with our own true values, identity and desires, and balanced for optimal well-being.

Furthermore, we can learn about and apply various tools and techniques (ancient as well as modern) in order to reduce individual stress and anxiety – working from the inside out so to process our traumas, reframe outdated thinking, reclaim our personal power and bring more peace and abundance into our lives.

This can allow us to be mindful, raise consciousness and align to our vibrational frequencies — the frequencies of our Energy System (the chakras) from which we operate, our emotions and the elements of Nature.

You can imagine how our body is made up of molecules which are vibrating constantly, like a kind of rhythm. Likewise, as for our bodies, rhythms happen on a grand scale too – like seasonal changes and tidal patterns. When balance is disturbed, natural rhythms are disrupted and become *dis-eased*. These changes on the larger scale then affect our collective and individual balance as well. The other way round, us raising our vibration individually and collectively, has a positive effect on the health of the world.

Seeing how our physical, emotional and spiritual health are intrinsically linked and how connecting and looking within can lead to our healing to lead to transformation, means we are awakening and reconnecting to our own life-force and spirit energy; individually and collectively.

I have applied various ancient as well as more modern natural healing tools and techniques throughout my own journey of self-discovery; my connection with nature and spirituality (not religion) has always been strong. However, I really started exploring the 'energy' world when I reached the age of about 24 (and it is forever continuing as I learn, grow and evolve).

Back then, an unsettling experience had left me unable to express how I really felt, but it wasn't until years later that I realised it had been this experience that nudged me towards opening up to my spiritual side, and really dealing with my emotions in a healthy way; through connecting, expressing and healing with the physical body so that feelings could flow.

I now know that there is a way to shift my inner state, and even to a whole new paradigm of living that doesn't require much effort other than just being myself!

Embodied Health

Our emotions are held in the body, and these become the tension in our muscles and the dis-eases we don't understand. I found that when I surrendered to my feelings, to sit with them, to allow them to be processed and integrated and released through my body in a healthy way, I would be given what I call a 'truth-chill' (a tingling) – it helps me to understand when something rings true for me. It feels like 'this is right'. It connects me with my inner knowing or intuition; with something that I need to hear, feel, see or sense at that moment in time and I must pay attention to it! It creates a better understanding of current situations and individual needs and desires, and helps in taking the next steps for our own transformation easier and actually joyful, even when we're coming through or out of unsettling or traumatic experiences.

An Embodied Health Approach asks us to address dis-ease, disability or illness experience by challenging science on etiology, diagnosis, treatment and prevention. It asks for a more holistic approach to include mental, emotional, physical, spiritual and relational health.

This is all so much part of my life now, as it helps me see the truth about who I am and how I fit into this world right now, and about where I want to see changes for a better world in the future. It is also how I build on my relationships, without wanting to react to others' opinions and behaviours, or feeling it is my responsibility to change or shape anyone else. Others too are allowed to be themselves, even if I feel they are not being true to themselves right now.

I don't know what they are holding on to or what their core beliefs are, but I feel they lack that mind-body-spirit and soul connection to help them shift their own inner and outer world for the better.

Religion Or Spirituality?

I'm sure you will have noticed that, maybe for about the past 2 generations, people do not (want to) identify with being 'religious' anymore. I have nothing against religion as such, because it all comes down to the initial value and highest vibration that we all crave and seek; Love. But as I see it, love is ever present, so we don't need to 'seek' it – we are spiritual beings in a human body, having a human experience, and we just need to open up to Love. Allowing ourselves to receive it. Lead with it in our work and in bringing up our offspring.

I feel that we are here to experience and to bring Love On Earth through ourselves. We all strive to have this in our life, but the thing is that we've already got it! We just end up blocking it. That can be for various reasons, e.g. due to early life experiences or (generational) trauma, abuse, a broken heart. We (often subconsciously) choose to push love away, because we may feel it is not going to last and so we're better off not having it at all. Blocking these emotions can allow for other emotions to take over; anger, resentment, guilt, shame, sadness.

However, if we can just allow ourselves to see the beauty, sweetness and abundance that life on Earth has to offer as well as how solitude and stillness can reconnect us to *self-love* at any time, we know that love is ever present.

Of course we will have those less happy and/or traumatising experiences of loss, abuse, loneliness and broken hearts, some people more or less than others (also depending on individual choices with respect to lifestyle).

However, it only stays a problem when we cannot move away from what is showing up in the present (our thoughts and behaviour) because we feel victimised from the past. We are, as a collective, becoming more and more aware that at the very core, *we are the source of our experiences on a behavioural level*. Shifting the consciousness of our core becomes the knowing that we are not alone in this, and we can shift those old, outdated, and self-sabotaging beliefs internally. It becomes the 'gold' that we can harvest to then pay it forward.

Coming back to religion as a way to live by, I feel that it is trying to rise above 'the earthly' - as if the Earth is where you've been placed *only* to suffer – to have a hard life – and then learn from that, as a general rehearsal for the afterlife. It is viewing nature and our natural instincts as primitive from which we are supposed to get away. Compared to spiritual beliefs in the way that witches, natural healers (energy workers, like myself) and shamans see these, nature, spirituality and earthly existence are actually embraced. We strive for a spiritual development with open eyes; not only with eyes closed in meditation or prayer. Nature's law is within our body, mind and soul; irrevocably, always. 'As above, so below'. We are part of nature. In fact, we *ARE* nature.

It was an eye-opener for me when my 'truth-chills' made me aware that God and Goddess / the Source / the Divine / the Energy or what you may like to call it, does not exist 'on the outside' somewhere or only 'up above', but is actually present in this world, and it makes you understand that 'a god' / 'goddess' etc. does not reign over the Earth, but IS the Earth.

We can lose our connection, hope or believe in ourselves or the Universe, but we can also restore it because we are not separated from the Godly or the Divine or Higher Source, and the Earth is not merely a 'front portal' of Heaven.

—

It is not so that The Godly and Holy only exist outside ourselves and our world and that only representatives of the faith are connected to the source. Believing that all of us can only be 'saved' or 'freed' if we lead a good life according to the rules of the religion, does not ring right to me. I feel that is a closed off and lonely existence, and it allows for the representatives of the faith to remain in control as their subjects need saving.

I consciously make choices in daily life about how I go about my day and interact with others. I don't come across as cynical or 'enlightened' and 'elevated' above the rest, because that is not the case and I am not in any way separate from anyone else. What I do is connect. I feel part of the whole and I have access to an endless source of love and information (as we all do). This is without hocus-pocus magic and needing 'sanctuary' or holiness. It is all about the experience, the essence. When you find that everything IS, in the present, everything can just BE. From this embodied space, it becomes more clear, natural and easy to make your truth informed choices.

For centuries, people have tried to connect - via religion and spiritual practices - with the power they feel within themselves and within nature.

It's all too easy to get confused and lost in these various practices, when it's not obvious that really all these roads lead to the same place and that the best and shortest route to the 'higher Power', or whatever you may like to call it, is a direct connection from within us. It's a knowing that this is always present, always readily available, and you can call on it whenever you need to. We are never alone, and always held.

So What About Current Reality?

Yes... what about reality in the world of today?

The fact is that 'money makes the world go round', as that is what we have created for ourselves! I would love to see money becoming an energy exchange again – that is how it is meant to work; it all began with our ancestors directly trading items and services.

In our world increasingly driven by technology, there is a real anxiety about what the future of money holds. However, it is clear that we all need to adapt to it to a certain extent. Societies are becoming cashless, and crypto-currency is becoming more mainstream, meaning the currencies aren't issued by a central authority so they can exist outside government interference or control. Governments in parts of the world are now offering Central Bank Digital Currency (CBDC) too, and these 'solutions' will play a role in what becomes of the banks and in how we interact with and use money in the future. To what extent and at what cost remains to be seen.

At this time in 2024, there is an obvious 'uprising' in our society, which has been going on for a few years now, as people are individually and collectively awakening to these truths and want to move away from the old that is hierarchical, racist, controlling and full of greed.

I am envisioning how we, as a community, will be able to support each other not only emotionally, but also with all of our shared resources. It needs to be understood that world-wide, not one agency or community is going to be able to support everyone. But we have connections and we can learn so much from each other – we don't need to keep re-inventing the wheel! I can see us rebuilding our community, and everywhere we are going to be looking at supporting each other with information learned, and how we can build those relationships to work together on the grand scale so that everyone benefits and the gap between rich and poor is bridged.

The Way Forward

All this is going to require many thoughts and actions, but thoughts themselves create our reality. We can only view the world through our own thoughts. We observe using our senses, but this information has to be processed by our minds and then be converted into thoughts, to allow us to understand this information. Thoughts contribute as much to reality as actions do.

The power of the mind is strong – you can actually stimulate the things you think about. Thinking one thing and doing another does therefore not work, and is why our wishes and desires will not come true if subconsciously our thoughts do not agree!

In my mentoring and embodiment work, being a Wellbeing Artist I use music/voice/sound, movement and art as a way to come home to self, and one of my main aims is to help others see the immense wealth of our planet we call Earth. We can learn and grow – climbing with the years and growing our self-confidence and self-worth.

Staying curious, exploring and wondering. Feeling the joy from it. We will fall and get back up; with integrity, lightness and a good sense of humour – because I believe that is what makes the world go round. It makes us irresistible and unbelievably inspiring.

Everything has its place and time; within Nature, the processes happen at their own pace and everything is as important as the other. The day is not more important than the night, ebb is not more important than flow, summer is not more important than winter. It is for us to find balance between our inner and outer world; male and female; body and mind; natural and supernatural; tangible and invisible; rest and action; dreaming away and being watchful; the Earth and the stars.

In our new Paradigm, I am seeing us letting go of our critical, analysing mind and allowing ourselves to simply BE more. Free and non-judgemental. Children being raised with these values and learning how to connect with nature from age 0. Pulling down that wall of words and intellectual knowledge between us and the world around us. I feel it's a transitioning into awakening and beyond; we are given the opportunity to experience the wonder all over again, as we **Lead with Love**.

Note by the lead author

Are you all spotting the links between the chapters yet?

Love. Connectedness.

The title of Femke's chapter says it all – Leading with Love, something that governments, heads of governments, (most) CEOs, and politicians seem totally incapable of doing!

She has a strong message of each of us learning that we are whole within ourselves and that we must listen (and act on) what our inner being tells us. How often have you gone against what your intuition has warned you about? Only to find yourself in a sticky situation that could have been avoided if you had followed your own warning!

And when we are truly complete within ourselves, the relationships we make with others are based on connection, respect, and mutual respect. They are not needy or demanding.

Femke believes, and I concur, that none of us were born onto this planet to accept suffering in the hope of a better religious afterlife. The fact that any belief system should perpetuate this is in order to control the very disciples it professes to love.

Love is never about control.

As Femke writes, none of us are separate from the divine (God, Universe, Higher Power) because the divine is within us all. We are all part of the source. Religious leaders and gurus are not the only people who can commune with the divine – everyone of us can.

There is also a strong message of connecting with nature in Femke's chapter, and she is right, we have a lot to learn by simply watching nature at work. Everything has a time, a place, and is never forced. Which feels to me like a great way to live our human lives.

This passage grabbed my attention: "At this time in 2024, there is an obvious 'uprising' in our society, which has been going on for a few years now, as people are individually and collectively awakening to these truths and want to move away from the old that is hierarchical, racist, controlling and full of greed."

It seems a fitting place to leave this recap.

Chapter 7

Our New World

by Natasha Shaw

Easing you, Empowering you, Unwinding you.

Freedom, Fulfilment, Flow, thriving in your loving, living and leading.

When we think about creating a 'New World', sometimes we can also have a sense of wondering when it will show up. And is it actually ever coming – Really!?

And the truth is. IT IS HERE NOW, RIGHT NOW and accessible AND

...... IT IS US.

Grounded us, part of our real lives and full of a frequency that is so much more expanded.

Consciously co-creating a new reality from my lived experience comes from playing in the intersection between our human life and our soulful layers, reconnecting to the subtle guidance sources within, so they become our discerning, trusted go to places. At the core, emphasising unity instead of division in both our inner and outer worlds.

And the more familiar those aspects of ourselves become, the easier it becomes to lean and flow with it all.

When I was younger, I remember feeling very connected to 'these ways' and then it was time to start school. And along came a sense of 'this is the way of life', so I thought I'd better get on with it. But at the same time, it all seemed so at odds. I wondered why the ways I remembered deep in the fabric of me, weren't being lived out in the 'real' world, when it meant you could create with ease and grace and not feel stressed and overwhelmed and there were support systems you could tap into. You didn't need to struggle to figure things out. So, what on earth was everybody up to and why had they forgotten? And then low and behold, I forgot too and yet I kinda didn't because I always had this annoying nag there was more to this world that I was supposed to be remembering without knowing what exactly it looked like and where on earth to find it. And that was a little crazy making! And my blessing in disguise, cos it constantly led me searching and researching, curious about so many things, in so many areas. The weird, the wonderful and the slightly insane!

Many years into my searching, in a daydream, a visual appeared. A cosy, inviting architecturally beautiful wooden barn lined at the far end with books all the way up to the ceiling. Knowledge and wisdom from floor to ceiling. Many people wandering in, conversing, light-hearted chit chatting everywhere. Laughter, vibrancy filling the air. Great food, warming drinks and space to be - sitting, absorbing and being whatever you needed to be in that space and moment.

The barn had two doors on either side. As you stood with the books behind you and looked all the way along to the other end, on the left, a small door came in from a colder, greyer world.

And directly opposite on the other wall, large sliding doors, headed straight out into a beautiful, reconnected world, the pace more at ease, a comfortable knowing that solving problems wasn't just done with the mind's capacity alone, relaxing you with that knowing. Here you flowed in and out with your own energy, no longer stuck on 'On' mode, recognising the movement staying still offered, easing you further and relaxing your overworked nervous system. And a vibrancy that filled your heart with so much joy of the vastness and interconnectedness that you were part of. Deeply alive and loving from an open heart. It was around the time of this daydream; that I met an amazing wisdom keeper who would become my mentor for the next 10+ years, helping me fully reconnect to what I had forgotten.

How passionate and filled up life feels experiencing how we return to what we always were. That greater, fuller spectrum. The opportunity to work in collaboration, connection, and communication with so many others also creating this way. This is the true experience of life for those resonating with that, and we're alive at a phenomenal time. To come in from one place and one way of being and shift into another way, with altered perspectives that completely reorientate us. Reconnecting us to the wider aspects of ourselves and our soulful as well as human layers. The 'New World' existing at the same time as the 'older' one, based on our choice point.

There is so much that is brand new for us. So we really are being it here for the first time, in our current capacity. On the one hand, that is awe inspiring and lights many of us up as it should, and it's also challenging as hell at times to go into new ways of being when we have known old ones for so, so long.

So always kindness, compassion and understanding towards ourselves.

How nuts is it, to add harshness and criticism instead?

Remembering we are human after all! And remembering that's the whole point of new, it's not familiar and so we practise new experiences until they become our go to ways. And to feel, know and trust the new for ourselves through our own lived experiences. As we all learn from each other.

Joyful, abundant, empowered, turning survive into thrive in all areas.

Dreaming Real - So we can begin to reconnect

We find ourselves in spaces that are inviting us to become more. As we live with our feet on the ground, this doesn't necessarily float along like ease and grace in our mental view of those words. It frequently looks like challenging or difficult situations. Maybe sadness, grief, anger, crappy things and dynamics, relationship issues, jobs etc, etc. They are the doors and we want to have some semblance of how on earth we open them to something more. I have so much respect for us human 'beings' because the higher aspects of us and wider information we have access to are not the part of us 'doing the doing', that's human us. Although the two of them are now going together to make up the whole. For example, I know when I'm moving through something with my husband, when a higher aspect of me has stepped in because I'm hearing information for the first time myself, about our situation that doesn't necessarily make sense to me but provides me with a higher perspective that my mind would never have known. And whilst brilliant, even with that, it's the two of us that then have to land it and integrate it into our lives for it to become real.

And it's messy and beautiful. And to witness the new human template coming online.

That's what we're all up to. **We are all co-creators creating, and this is how we're doing it**. To me, it's ballsy, powerful, strong. It takes courage!

And also, sometimes we get to come at it out of the pure joy of a new creation and we simply arrive. Plonk! Wonderful! But that's not really what I'm wanting to speak about because, for many, these ways are only just landing, so as we become more familiar with them, they will naturally and organically shift to the full new potential.

And so, it is our felt perception that is the real door opener.

I AM Present to What is

As we begin to feel what's true for us, given that more often than not, it is the grey tones that bring us in, the ability to be present to what is, can take a little bit of re-calibration. It's familiar to not entirely know what we are actually feeling beyond the content that is playing out. It's also very familiar that if we do go anywhere near it, we don't like how it feels, and so the usual narrative is to ask, 'what can I do to make the feeling better or go away?' This is a separation energy, and when we look to solve something, fix, or change it before we have engaged our 'higher' aspects and our wider perspective, we miss the full capacity of the opportunity. The paradox is that sadness is sadness, anger is anger. Rage is rage. Grief is grief. Tears of pain are painful. And that also, in their pure form, they form some of the most potent energies of creation we have.

So we begin by asking ourselves, where am I in truth right now? I want you to imagine an infinity loop. On one side is your inner landscape and on the other is your outer landscape. They are one and the same thing, as what you are feeling on the inside is what you will be emitting on the outside.

Right in the middle, where the two points meet, is your resonant frequency, i.e. the match to what you are really feeling and therefore emitting, regardless of whether you like it or not and whether you are conscious of it or not! So the beginning point is identifying what this actually is in truth, or the truth of who you really are at that given moment in time. The point in the middle is either going to be transmitting a discordant or a coherent or more harmonic frequency.

And this is the true essence of the vibrational frequency you are emitting into the field, like a wave form that moves out of us. Sound frequency is a beautiful way to see visually coherent or discordant patterns, where sound vibration is made visible, for example, by putting it into water molecules. Check out John Stuart Reid's work on sound cymatics. All the cells in our body are vibrating and sound, electromagnetic and light energy can all travel outside of the confines of our skin. And so even in silence, we are still communicating a frequency of energy that is noticed at the level of felt perception by others.

Jill Bolte Tylor, a famous neuroscientist, gives us a brilliant illustration of this. In 1996, she suffered a severe haemorrhage and because of her medical knowledge of the brain, she watched as the left-hand brain functions began to shut down. That afternoon, she lost the ability to walk, talk, read, write, or recall any of her life. What happened in the process was that the right side of her brain came online in a massive way. Her felt perception.

In the hospital, she became aware of how people were treating her. Jill could no longer understand words, let alone remember who people were, and she talks about how the energy people were carrying became very obvious. She didn't recognise her own mum.

She didn't even have a concept for what a mum was. But she knew the lady who would climb up onto her bed and sit with, cared deeply. She knew how all the people interacting with her were showing up. And she goes on to discuss that it was only those showing deep love, care and compassion that she wanted to respond to. Those without heart, it felt too challenging for her to make the effort to recover. 8 years later, Jill made a full recovery and now teaches and speaks to millions of people about the importance of the energy we are bringing to any situation. And that goes just as much to ourselves and how we are showing up on the inside.

Many years ago, my mentor would say, (from the collective consciousness of the children), "**We don't care how you feel, we care that you know how you feel".** My goodness, what a powerful message this has been!

Because this is what is really being received, this is where the greatest capacity for change lies in our inner landscape and **then the frequency you are emitting has the power to unify both internally and externally.** This is the true power to transform, the power to heal, the power to take accountable. And so with everything as a felt perception and energy in motion. We focus there.

Where are we really? What energy? What frequency are you really running? It brings a whole new meaning to the phrase "Look at the state you're in!".

The beautiful Rumi quote, "Between right and wrong there is a field, I'll meet you there", is such a brilliant reminder of how we can learn to show up to ourselves and others. It shifts our perspective on judging our feelings as good or bad. From another vantage point, they are exactly what we need, despite the fact they may not feel 'good'!

Instead, cultivating a still point that is about being loving, kind and compassionate to ourselves, and our capacity to hold all we are feeling, allowing the presence of it all, is the way through. Allowing it to exist supports unifying it, rather than dividing a part of ourselves away from ourselves. And that's key. No force, no pushing to change. Energy has a movement all of its own and when you allow it to flow, it's beautiful and informative and moves. Don't stand in a flowing river and try to turn around and hold yourself against the tide. Stand in its direction and flow with it. You will move so much faster that way, carrying the energies of love and connection as you go. And accessing your clarity and wisdom.

I cannot tell you the number of times I have, through instinct to avoid discomfort or pain, moved away from feeling. Only to recognise later, that had I not allowed that integration to exist, I could not have heard what was beyond it. The deep wisdom that's held there. And I never would have imagined or mentally figured out those what I often hear or become aware of, especially with our wonderfully active mental capacity to problem solve. The whole process is the reconnection, and so, without one step, the next cannot exist because you are transforming and becoming with each step.

We get to see it, we get to witness it, we get to observe what our patterns of creation have looked like up to this point. That is powerful! Always adding love, compassion and understanding for our wholeness. Remember these patterns, imprints and programming have been there for a long, long time.

So we…
Are present to;
Value and allow what comes up to 'simply' be there.

As part of energy in motion, as part of a greater whole and a wider perspective unfolding in present moment time.

Then we can sit in the stillness of the experience. The chaos and the calm simultaneously existing and beyond that, through the eye of the storm, into the wisdom and clarity that resides there and wants to flow through you, with you, as you.

I AM IN COMPLETE ALLOWANCE OF RECEIVERSHIP

I invite you to say the above out loud to yourself.

Around creation, we have been familiar with looking to fix and solve things with our mind's left-brain capacity alone. We are programmed that in order to do anything effectively it requires hard work and "efforting". How could we achieve and have anything arrive with ease and grace? That is simply not a thing. We can feel it doesn't seem possible for it to happen. Or we go into a whirlwind of mentally figuring out what we need to do, to make it happen or to fix our current state. Essentially, what do I need to do to solve it? And fast! And worry, stress and low-level anxiety, the denser energies get activated. Based on what we have often lived to this point. It's been real. We have known many, many experiences of things not coming along. And the energetics of the planet were not what they currently are. Let's acknowledge that it's been challenging and exhausting. And now we go to our still point.

And we remember connected to our wider aspects, tools and techniques are not static, they offer real time information, present moment feedback loops that are orchestrated with precision for what unfolds. So you get to live both in rest and ease whilst equally moving forwards without the need to stretch your mind into stress. Creating far beyond what you would have created with hard work, sheer slog and straining, and over thinking.

Through reconnecting to higher levels of consciousness, there are many, many more systems available to us to tap into. It's exciting to see all of our innate capabilities and capacities come back online for our own and others' expansion. And that this is going to continue to develop throughout our lives. We can still put the doing in, but it's a different kind. Its direction has come out of inspired action and our inner knowing of a direction to take. It has come out of the stillness we created to listen to our inner voice and knowing without push, pull or force.

I invite you again to read the following phrase out loud. "I AM in complete allowance of receivership". As if it was your birth right because it is.

And this time, notice what you notice. There may be aspects that are fully on board and aspects that go "no I am not! I have never been provided for, I don't trust the process, it's all BS anyway"…etc, etc.

And you know what to do. Go into your body and allow what's there to be. Offering love and patience and acceptance. No need to kick it out. No need to force anything to believe anything. And the cool thing is we're going there anyway, even with the parts of us that aren't on board. Then beyond that space we can hear the higher perspectives. That then has space to come into us. And instead of jumping into action, we can jump into stillness. And be open to receive. It always comes.

Also, our nervous system in the face of something to fix or solve, has been very familiar with a buzz energy and so when we go to stillness and not doing, solving, fixing, busying, the mind can perceive the stillness as if something's wrong. If we go into a sense of 'not worrying', it signals we're not doing what we 'should' be doing and that can kick up anxiety.

So be easy on yourselves, remind your mind, it doesn't have to do it alone. It is not that nothing is being done, it is that it is being done in a new way, an unfamiliar way. Remind your mind that there is a great deal of inner and outer dimensional connectedness that has your back and is giving you the support of a souped-up AI level next generation capacity. Ask for something to show up, to help you see and know this for yourself. And once again be open to receive, giving up the how, what, where, why, and who it will be done with, the mental mind loves that stuff and instead move into being present with whatever unfolds in front of you and remember this is exactly how it is meant to unfold for you. Return to stillness, joy, ease, taking care of yourself, or doing something fun.

Begin to bank the experiences of how life can unfold in these new ways, and you will start to notice them in greater and greater experiences of your life. Release the desire for outcomes and instead begin to feel the awe of the ride, to know that you have already chosen, and each day is about the practise of these ways, like a curious child learning, reconnecting and recalibrating. You are already there each day you orientate that way, not where to get to, you already arrived. And it is also coming towards you.

Imagine knowing that creating rest, relaxation, joy and self-care are the new ways of creating. Setting your energy there and not in crazy over-do mode is actually how we can roll. And we'll have plenty of sprinkles of stress, worry, concern if we want it; it can come along for the ride if it wants to. Always remember love, compassion and understanding for all that arises. It will do your energy field the world of good. And all the while, inner knowing and infinite sources of information are becoming more and more the way you flow.

And remembering that when things look like they are dismantling and going 'wrong' or feeling rubbish, that is so much a part of the process, it's part of the whole of the orchestration. It's often what we put into motion in the first place and then forgot the dismantling was part of it. So, it allows us to move our compassion into a more spherical perspective of what 'good' and 'bad', right and wrong, positive and negative, actually are. What we perceive as coming up that is causing us a problem and not representative of ease and grace is exactly the next experience we need to be in, to create the whole that we are moving towards. It's easy not to remember the presence of the whole. Another expression of how the infinity loop actually works.

Given the massive re-orientation that moving through something can be, it can be very tiring. The mental mind might have created a rosy picture of floating along on clouds and a calm, beautiful serenity unfolding everything. And it can be, and that's wonderful if it is. But if the reality is a little bit crazy making sometimes, remember being here right now in all the chaos creating new ways, is like setting up a space station in your kitchen. Your once cosy central hub, where everyone milled and passed through as you cooked food, has now been taken over with a lot of new devices powering up and making the space all tight and complicated and messy and noisy and anything but calm. New wiring, new pathways, new emotions in the space. So, to our love of knowing, controlling, planning, not trusting the unknown, let's give all that love, compassion, and patience. We are being supported by phenomenal sources and we 'simply' chose to arrive in more and more of our freedom, fulfilment, flow and soulful energy, and then we unfold into our next now moment. Present, present, present to what is. Self-care and kindness to everything that arises.

New ways

New possibilities

New World

It is my deepest wish for as many of us as possible to find our way back to more and more of the wider capacity we hold, the greater truth of who we really are. So that we are empowered to transform the way we live, love, and lead. And so that we can do it with as much ease and grace to ourselves as we go.

To living the rest of our lives

Bigger – Brighter – Bolder

Note by the lead author

In contrast to some of the other chapters, Natasha's seems very mystical to me, very deep, causing me to pause and reflect on her words.

Which, when you think about it, is exactly what she is saying throughout her writing. She is inviting us to look inside, be calm, be still, and listen to our innate wisdom. We all have it, the power to transform ourselves, and by example, other people and the wider world. The problem is, we are all so busy dealing with our outward facing life that we neglect our inner being.

I particularly like her emphasis on the importance of letting go of outcomes, and how, why, and when something will happen. And instead of forcing something into existence, simply allowing it to be. In our current frenetic, 24/7 way of life, this probably seems like an impossibility...I mean, how can you be successful, have lots of money etc., unless you push and strive? Natasha thinks you can have what you need and desire, by working with your thoughts and feelings, aligning to your energy, and just BEing – and so do I.

Learning to think and be in this new way is not going to be easy for everyone. There will always be people who want more, believe they deserve more than everyone else, and they are not afraid to push others aside, steal, hurt, lie and deceive. These kinds of people also tend to want to be the centre of attention – if we stop giving it (attention) to them, if they lose their audience, then maybe, just maybe, they will begin to do the inner work on themselves!

We can live in hope.

Chapter 8

Within My Heart

by Nikki Baker

The large tent-like structure billows forward in the breeze. A crimson flash of promise reveals its entrance into a realm I have always wished to visit.

I wait patiently in line as, one by one, people step over the threshold into the world they most desire. How many versions of this would there be, I wonder, or do we all fundamentally at heart wish for the same thing?

I step forward knowing there is no return, no safety net of the life I know. With this thought comes the realisation that what I want comes with the bravery of facing the untravelled, the unlearnt, the unfamiliar route. I feel I have always needed to discover this to find true inner peace, but right now, as my turn edges closer, I feel anything but peaceful inside.

I take a deep breath in and another step forward. I reach out and cautiously part the bold coloured entrance. The material feels softer, more yielding than it looks. I relax, just a little.

A light but certain breeze catches the fabric and brushes it against me, turning my white dress instantly gold.

I feel a warm shiver from the back of my heels, which tingles all the way up to the top of my spine. I take one more step.

A warm, certain glow powerfully fills my heart as I allow the curtains to drape closed behind me.

My fear begins to dissipate.

For a moment, I cannot see. The bright glare of the Autumnal sunshine cut dead as the curtains close on the world I know.

Final.

Stepping back is no longer an option, no longer fitting for me anyway.

I stand motionless for a moment and close my eyes, trying to feel the energy surrounding me. The crimson of my eyelids mimics the colour I met upon entering this place. It startles me into opening my eyes again.

Now I see…

All around me, a fire glow of amber, flame like but not emanating from any source. It flickers along the floor, lapping around my ankles.

No heat, no sound, just colour.

In front of me is a large round cherry wood table. A silky-rich auburn blanket casually draped over it. Stroking the ground in places, it merges into the orange glow of the floor.

I feel heat rising and resting within my womb.

I blink several times to try and take it all in, and as I do I feel a gentle but certain force push me forwards toward the chair in front of the table. I steady myself, placing my hand firmly on the back of it. I do not want to stumble, not now. I need support as I look around to confirm the scene unfolding before me, feeling vulnerable to what lies ahead.

The wood feels smooth and somehow acquiescent under my touch, like the gentle, solid foundation of a trusted friendship.

As I pull out the chair and gravitate towards sitting on it, I notice a woman opposite me, mirroring my action to sit.

Upon the chair seat is a glowing yellow cushion, appearing to almost sparkle with energy. I take my seat upon it, settle into its warmth, and hold my breath just long enough to feel my heart pound loudly.

Where will this journey take me?

In the middle of the table, a head-sized crystal ball sits proudly. Mystical swirls of unfathomable colours mesmerise me deeper into its world.

Then the woman speaks, gentle but sure.

"Place your hands on either side and let your heart guide you."

I am already instinctively reaching forward to touch the sphere as she speaks.

The woman smiles with her emerald green eyes fully focused on me. I feel she can see into my soul, and I sense my energy rise as I connect to the vibrant orb on the table.

"Your heart will tell you what you need," she continues, "close your eyes and feel it speak."

I do as she says and allow myself to let go of any apprehensions. I give myself fully to the present situation and as I do, I hear myself say out loud,

"Trust the process.".

I feel a strong gust of air, more forceful than the one when I entered this new domain. At the same time, nothing moves. My skin cools and I am suddenly transported back to myself as a child.

Four years old, alone, scared and confused. What has happened, and why does everyone seem so angry at me? The sadness is suffocating, a cloak of unspoken trauma drawn tight.

"I'm sorry," I hear myself say. "Do you still love me?"

There is another stronger force of atmosphere, stormier than before, but again it seems almost to be coming from within me.

The room remains statue still.

Then the whole world seems to suddenly swirl in a deep dark navy blue and I'm moving forward, swaying as the energy in my body stirs me. My cheeks feel wet and cold against the warmth of where I'm sitting.

I feel an oppressive air in my being as my teenage self appears before me. She is hurt, angry, feeling misunderstood, and painfully shy. Fearing myself, my emotions, my power; best to be small, not say how I truly feel. There are many ways to numb any feelings, soak them all up, take them all in and hide them; just do not ask for what I want. Who am I to ask for what I want?

I feel a chill hit me with a force that makes me inhale sharply. I now see the young woman this lost girl becomes standing in front of me. The darkness of the world I have created, the path I have carved from the unloved, unseen depths of what I have grown to call my world. She is too frightened to ask for what she needs, too 'strong' to connect to her vulnerability. Swirling fast and furiously now in a pool of dark indigo, I can see something brightening within the depths of all that swallows her up.

Reaching out, I want to hold her, but I cannot touch her. Her journey is not yet over.

I can sense the woman looking at me, but I cannot open my eyes. I'm too fearful I may lose where I am; too entrenched to pull back, however dark this is feeling.

Is this my world? Is this what's in my heart?

As I think it, I must say it out loud as the woman answers the question.

"Everything is in your heart."

The room is still lingering blue, but this colour is fading; everything seems to be fading. I can feel my energy weakening and my breath getting shallower.

I feel like I am rushing forwards and rushing backwards all at once. In the disorientation of it all, a mix of emotions floods my body, and I cry out.

No words, just sound, like a wounded animal calling for its tribe.

Black and white flashes sear across my eyelids as I feel myself slump in the chair.

Everything is still for a moment, stopped in time, but which time I do not know.

And then I see myself, holding my one and only baby. She looks at me, and I know she is the answer. Something in me just knows.

Everything that has gone before has gone before for this moment. Something bigger than me, something I can hold, cherish, and love forever.

A warm cloak of purple velvet envelops itself around us as we breathe each other in for the first time.

I feel safe; she is safe.

For a moment, a recognition of what I can and have created overwhelms me.

This is the cycle of the world, and I have been awakened to the knowledge of my true contribution to it. Playing small does not serve the universe.

I'm here to help raise the energetic vibration of the world as a whole, and this will be my new world, her new world.

I understand that now.

I feel my soul lift out of my body, and I can sense a lightness all around. My energy returns with such a strong sense of comprehension. I feel myself melting back into the chair.

The colours calm, all confusion fades. Peace resides.

I open my eyes and the woman is no longer in front of me; but instead, I am looking directly into a large mirror. It is beautifully ornate in silver gilt. A collection of memento mori decorates its borders; winged cherubs cascading amongst half-filled hours of glasses and crystal sparkling skulls.

Tumbling token reminders of our inevitable flesh and bone mortality.

What I see facing me in the mirror makes me cry.

I see all aspects of the girl I have been, the child, the teenager, the young woman… all the way up to the present…and then somehow beyond, which does not scare me like it used to.

I see the woman again, looking back at me now. She is beckoning me to continue my journey. Her green eyes smile knowingly, and I recognise she is my Inner Mentor.

She is there to guide me, giving clarification that the world I wish to be in is the world that already exists within me.

She speaks once more.

"The world you wish for is waiting within; it lives within your heart. You have the power to create it all; you always have done."

It is a world that is ultimately full of love. Self-love, love for others, love for the world. But how do I recognise love without pain, sadness, loss, trauma? The world I am searching for is not actually a world devoid of these things; it is a world that learns from these things, *truly* learns.

This life is here to teach me this. I am ready. I accept this.

An understanding that this earthly life is only the beginning and is here to test me and guide me to a truly energetic resonance with love, a love that will take me over the threshold into the true world I am ultimately meant to be part of.

I feel I am crossing a threshold that was always waiting for me.

Every step in the journey of my life has been exactly what it was meant to be to prepare me.

I understand this now.

I feel like I could fly, and I feel like I now take up the space I was always meant to fill. I am part of the new world's message, part of the movement that will change the world forever.

Human suffering is part of human growth, the human experience; but we are more, much more than just humans.

It is our soul's purpose to provide the new world we want from the teachings and learnings undertaken in our human form, in our hearts.

I have, we have, the power to choose how to use our energy for good or bad. We have a human lifetime to connect to the energetic vibration that we feel serves us and the world best.

This is the journey; this is the new world.

Not all will choose a high frequency on this voyage and there will be a divide beyond each of our mortal lives with a mixture of energies left in their wake. So, the cycle continues until all the energies can resonate from the highest vibrational frequency.

Now I know that to embrace this truer world, I need to re-awaken within my earthly life. I must embrace the self-love necessary to truly take love out into the world, to lift the vibration of its energy, to heal. This is not a lone quest; it comes from within us all.

I close my eyes and breathe in deeply.

I open my eyes and I am out in the world again, but it is not the world I left. I am not the same person; everything feels different now.

I understand my journey and the world I am creating. It's a collective individualisation to raise the vibrational energy of the world. A collective consciousness.

This is each soul's purpose. This will create the New World.

It is time and I am ready; the world is ready too.

I don't look back. As I step forward, my dress turns from gold to white, but it is not the same white as before. It has a clarity and purity, an outwards reflection of my inner transformation.

Note by the lead author

I love the dreamy, descriptive nature of Nikki's contribution. In the same way as Natasha, she is looking inside herself for the answers.

Nikki talks about "awakening", something that is frequently talked about in "woo woo" circles, and often in a way that separates those "awakened" souls from everyone else. It's a kind of spiritual elitism that doesn't do anyone any good, instead it creates yet another "them and us" scenario in a world already full of them! In contrast, she describes "awakening" as being something individual, inferring that every single person has the opportunity to move into a new way of being and embrace a new way of living on this planet.

She also touches on the fact that there are, and will be, different levels of human energetic frequencies, but that ultimately, the goal is that every one of us reaches the highest level of energetic frequency – that of LOVE.

This chapter has a strong theme of collaboration and collective thinking – literally the personification of the subtitle of this book – "Consciously co-creating a new reality". It's almost as if we planned it <grin>.

Out of many gems, one of the quotes that resonated very strongly with me is: "It is our soul's purpose to provide the new world we want from the teachings and learnings undertaken in our human form, in our hearts."

I invite you to pick a line, a sentence, that speaks to your heart – that is the message you need to take from Nikki's work.

Chapter 9

The New Paradigm is Closer Than You Think

by Ramona Stronach

You

Do you believe you have the power to shape the world's future? Do you believe you have the power to change your life? Believe it or not, the two go hand in hand because you are pure energy, and your energy is connected to everything. I am betting a lot of naysaying voices flooded up within you with their associated feelings of doubt, cynicism, despair, etc. That's okay; none of these are the truth of who you are.

We have widely been led to *believe* we are insignificant and do not make a difference to the world's negative paradigms. Our limiting beliefs about ourselves have made many feel powerless in the face of a seemingly chaotic world.

We live within systems (for decades, even centuries) that have *disconnected us from tuning within* to our true voice, our centre of direction if you like, and it is time to reclaim ourselves back - reconnecting to who we are beyond the world's paradigms and our individual paradigms because we are not insignificant whatsoever. We can heal our minds and shift what we project out onto the world, which changes our experience of life. We can heal our bodies and each other, tap into intuition and wisdom, and positively affect energy fields. We matter very much to the shaping of the future on this Earth.

When we realise our life is shaped by beliefs that keep us stuck and small, we begin to perceive the external world in a different light because our *consciousness* up-levels; we start to see through inauthenticity, controlling paradigms and manipulative narratives or discourses. When this happens, we cannot unsee, and something stirs deep within us that tells us something is iniquitous.

This stirring deep within is the momentum for re-attuning to who we really are. *It is the call that brings us back into ourselves*. It is the first step to trailblazing new life affirming paradigms for ourselves and the world. *You are* the new paradigm for an amazing future, believe it or not, and you are incredibly important because you are here on planet Earth - because you are You.

Reality

If you have ever felt there has to be more to this 'reality' you find yourself within, you are already tuned in to the fact that there is most definitely more to it than we perceive with our senses. You have begun to get curious and started awakening to seeing and *feeling* beyond the conditioning that the world has imposed upon you; you are more than just matter – you are a multi-dimensional energy Being.

Take a moment to reflect on the narratives that are influencing people's perception of their own reality – the 'not enough to go around' or, 'there is only one winner' or, 'for the greater good' or, 'there is only one way'. Can you feel the energy of conflict, competition, and separation within these narratives? Do you find that you are experiencing this reality? When did we sign up to believe these? Is this the reality we want to continue believing in?

Is this the future we envision for ourselves, our loved ones and our world – one of scarcity, conflict and division?

No doubt, many times, you will have felt completely powerless when you have looked upon the world with a huge heart full of dismay. You will have likely felt on a treadmill. Maybe you have felt overwhelming emptiness, continual stress or an anxious sense that there is no time for anything. These are all indications that the current paradigms on Earth are not working for us. And *thank goodness* for these heavy and dense feelings because they are our cues, prompting us to go within to find our centre point – our place of stillness and our true guidance. It is an invite to get curious and think *critically* about everything we *have been* and *are still being told* by the external world about what we should be, do or have.

After all, systems, structures, paradigms, narratives, discourses, regimes, etc., *can only exist* when the populations of the world listen to them, live them, use them, buy them, support them, comply or adhere to them. And if we do subscribe, we make no room for a different reality to emerge, and our true potential as human beings will continue to be suppressed. Do we want this for our future generations?

Outer and Inner Paradigms

If you look into the meanings ascribed to the word paradigm, the words "pattern", "way of doing something", and "system of beliefs" are all attached to it. It is evident that in the world we look upon, the paradigms we currently live within are of the low vibrational kind. The energies of these paradigms influence populations on both the conscious and subconscious levels to view the world through the perception of fear, division, separateness, individualism, competition, and conflict, either subtly or directly, through varying channels.

127

On the inner level, our own personal paradigms can feed into external paradigms and we can end up reinforcing them through our *perception* or projection. How does this happen? The subconscious mind.

When we are in the development stages from conception to 6 years of age, we form perceptions – beliefs – about ourselves and the world, and our subconscious mind records everything because its job is to protect us. Depending upon how positive our early childhood life experiences were and how we were supported to feel all of our feelings (process them) determines how our beliefs serve us or not in adult life.

As we move through time space, the subconscious mind continues to fulfil its protective role and seeks out any information it can from the outside world (anything and everything outside of us) to validate our early formed beliefs and life perceptions – whether positive or negative.

Let's take a quick example to illustrate the power of the subconscious mind feeding into the negative paradigm of competition ("survival of the fittest" narrative); our younger self forms a core belief that life is hard because of our early years environment and upbringing. The subconscious mind will 'look' for anything to affirm this belief that it recorded as we move through life, including the paradigms and narratives of the world that align with this belief.

Subsequently, we may find our general experience of life in adulthood is a struggle - especially to experience what we desire - because our core belief is that life is hard.

We may find ourselves in situations where we experience competition that doesn't make us feel good, as opposed to circumstances where we are encouraged and supported because of our subconscious beliefs.

All of which put us in an energetic stance where we block what we would love to experience materialising for us. There is, of course, a much more complex 'mirroring' relationship between our inner and outer world on the subconscious level than this simple example. The key takeaway here is to understand the powerful nature of the subconscious mind that runs our show for 95% of the day; that is a lot of time during our day when we are running off subconscious beliefs, especially if they are predominantly negative.

How do we know what our subconscious negative beliefs are that form our own internal controlling paradigms? *Our feelings are the clue.*

And how many of us allow ourselves to be distracted away from feeling our painful emotions due to the design of the systems we live within keeping us hooked into repeat cycles of ways of being? The packaging of the external world – for example, retail therapy, 'smart' phones, celebrity culture, highly addictive sugary processed foods, alcohol, offers galore, altered states of consciousness to relax us and make us feel good, television, social media – it goes on – makes it look like the majority of humans are living their best life, but on deeper reflection, do these things really support human freedom?

Do they support us to live our true amazing potential? Not to mention the huge profit corporate companies make from offering people (often unhealthy) distraction from who they really are.

Yes, anything but gift ourselves our own attention because it is too painful to go within and embrace our patterns of shame, self-hate, pity, jealousy, anger, you name it. And these patterns can be undone to set ourselves free.

The Bottom Line of the World's Paradigms - Fear

Have you ever wondered why the external world seems to be set up to create fear? Let's look at some examples: fear of not being able to pay bills, fear of losing your home, fear of something happening by so-called 'terrorists', fear of becoming ill (remember the 1 in 3 will get cancer advertisement in the UK?), fear of being laid off work, fear that you will be sued, fear of wars, fear of losing business, fear you will lose money, fear there are not enough resources to go around, fear there are just too many humans on Earth, fear of the weather, fear of what others might say about you if you stand up to something unethical, fear of being late for work, fear of being alone, fear of crime – the list seems endless.

So what is this fear paradigm engendered in many aspects of modern life all about?

For starters, the world wants *our attention*. Let's rephrase that: the few who own the majority of the world's wealth want our attention. Attention is the new currency. And what gets people's attention immediately?

Fear.

When people are in fear, it places them in the right energetic space for control and coercion and crucially it is a distraction technique. They are likely to act from a place of fear rather than listen to *their own truth and authority*.

When we are distracted from ourselves, we are in an easier position for manipulation. When our attention is diverted away from within ourselves, we lose touch with that incredible wise part of us that *intuitively* knows when truth is not being told. And the modern world has done a great job of dismissing human intuition – intuition is powerful.

If we didn't buy into the outlets used to create fear and which change behaviour and influence mindset – television, news, media, advertising etc., the fear agenda would simply stop.

Imagine; we would connect more to family and community – and families and communities are a very powerful force. We would have a stronger connection to All things Nature because we would realise we *are nature*. We would simply say no to bodies of people and corporate companies who make decisions and take actions that are harmful without our consent. We would take full control of our own health and our mental well-being. We would self-direct ourselves. I believe that we would experience a very different reality for ourselves and the world. We would use our consciousness more wisely.

Yet, we do have control over what we do with the feelings of fear when it lands in our body systems from the external world. When we feel fear (conditioning), the kindest paradigms we can act within are self-compassion, self-love for the very essence of ourselves and acknowledgement of how we feel. This is critical to help discharge the emotions through the body systems so we don't suppress them.

We can then look at what the fear brings up for us on the personal level; what meaning do we ascribe it? There will be a subconscious or conscious belief underlying the fear we feel. We then can *choose* to believe in what has caused us fear and fuel it by giving it our energy and attention and enslaving ourselves to whatever is behind the fear – whether that be a narrative, a system, a movement, technology, etc. Or we can simply say no thank you and turn away from it. We should never underestimate the power of simply saying no.

Let's bring this up close and personal. You may remember an occasion where you experienced a strict teacher, parent or some authority figure that triggered feelings of fear within you to get you to comply or behave. If this was unexpected and you felt isolated in addition to the dramatic nature of being put into fear mode, you will likely have formed a belief associated with the traumatic element of this experience. Fast forward to your adult life, and you hear something from an 'authority' figure; you immediately adhere to it without question, regardless of how negative or positive it is. In other words, you are immediately *back in the energy of that fear state*. In this energetic state, you cannot think critically and you cannot feel or hear your true voice guiding you and you are at risk of supporting something that is not for humanity's interests.

This is how the subconscious mind can run the show, and we make decisions from the space of fight or flight if we don't give ourselves time to feel the fear, process it (the emotional charge dissipates through the body systems) and release ourselves from its grip through resolution.

Resolution here means *looking at the perception you made as a child in a different way.*

When resolution is obtained from our childhood traumas, the energy we were trapped within no longer has a hold on us and we can make decisions about what the world tells us from a neutral and wise space; we can listen and trust *our own authority*.

We would not have made the connection between our reaction to adhering to an 'authority figure' as an adult and that traumatic event with the strict authority figure all those years ago with the conscious mind.

Remember, the subconscious mind's job is to protect you, but we need to override it because what it recorded in childhood *no longer serves us as adults*.

When the mind controls us with fear mongering thoughts, we can't tune into logic or common sense, never mind our wisdom, because the body's resources are dealing with fight or flight energy – and that is where we get into trouble as human beings in the modern world. The proverbial tiger has been replaced with paradigms which you can choose to be in fear of or not. This is the relational aspect of our inner world with the outer world.

If you are feeling lost about the seeming chaos the outer world is reflecting back to you, if you are feeling any despair, low feelings, hopelessness, or fear, know these are messages for you to go within yourself. They are inviting you to take the inner journey to who you really are beyond the conditioned mind the world created and shift your old perceptions about yourself to create new life affirming paradigms.

So 'how on 'earth' do we have the power to redefine new paradigms, I hear you say? *It is awareness that births new consciousness that changes what we project onto our own life and the world.*

Awareness Births New Consciousness

Awareness is the starting point for the expansion of our own consciousness. When we are aware of our own painful patterns as they come up in the moment for us, this is good news as it means *something in our minds needs healing, a shift in our self-perception* - even though it certainly does not feel anything could be remotely good from the intense feelings that can painfully flood up.

Remember that, largely, we have been taught pain is something to be feared. We need to reassure our nervous system it is safe to feel emotional pain. We need to reassure that younger self of ours that they are safe, we have got their back and it is okay to let go.

Awareness of our inner state when we take actions relating to decisions we make in our lives is critical because we often *think* we are making them independently for ourselves. But consider this: behind all the narratives in our mind lie beliefs, and underneath these beliefs is usually a voice that very often does not belong to you. You will know it's not your own true voice because your body will let you know; your energy will feel contracted when you make the decision or take the action.

Let's take the mental body, those voices in your mind – the ones that hold you back and berate you. These are not your truth. They belong to others who had a role in your upbringing, and your environment. In fact, you can bet that the voices do not belong to those people either. They have likely been passed down the ancestral line without question. We need to get intimate with our own true voice, and that means accepting ALL of our parts – yes, even those parts that have terrible voices that do not say loving things to us.

It then becomes easier to discern the not-so-authentic voices (narratives) of anyone outside of you, from those close to you, to voices attached to bodies of people that govern, provide services, public information and so forth. We can then tune into what *feels right, whole and expansive* to us in any given moment. And we can take action from *this energetic space that is aligned with us* and not somebody else's contracted energetic space.

This is how we shape the future – *by looking within ourselves.* And when we start to heal our mind from negative patterns, we subconsciously give others permission to do the same because science is demonstrating that we are all connected to an incredible field of energy – ancient knowledge that humans have always known, but the perpetuation of negative paradigms has separated us from.

When our consciousness expands, we *naturally make conscious choices* about what we engage with, interact with, what we support and allow to come into our physical life, our physical body, and our subconscious mind from the external world.

When we cultivate awareness of our patterns that berate us, hurt us, intimidate us, coerce us, and so much more, we begin to become conscious of the world's paradigms, systems, structures, narratives and so forth that do the same, and we see through them immediately.

We are the consciousness behind the patterns, though our conditioning would have us believe we are the patterns themselves. And we are beginning to tune into how powerful consciousness is when we direct it with specific intentions for ourselves or others.

Freeing Ourselves from the Conditioned Mind

Every single thing in our lives is mirroring back to us whether we are slave to our conditioned mind or not. Our thoughts come and go, yet some take hold of us in excruciating ways and dictate, demand and control us. When we can learn to be aware of these thoughts and not get caught up in their firm grip, we release their energy.

We learn we have a choice not to identify with them and can begin to change the relationship to our thoughts. We experience that we are *not the thoughts* but the incredible consciousness behind them.

When you begin to free yourself from the conditioned mind paradigms, you do not see things in the same light – literally. You are light itself, and you will see life through this *real light* you are made of.

You will feel lighter within, and the expansive feeling we experience when we release stuck energy lets us know we have connected back to our light.

This is a powerful light indeed, and you will find yourself backing You up, setting your boundaries and saying no to anything that does not resonate with your energy and align with your truth.

You will start to discern more wisely when it comes to the business of anything external that tells you what to do or not do and has an inauthentic energy about it. You will question what you hear and see, and more importantly, you will feel into its truth or not. You will start to trust yourself more and follow your own energy, and this is immensely liberating.

Imagine a world where people stood up to their own conditioning and freed themselves. Now imagine this in the external. The world's harmful paradigms would crumble because no one would subscribe to them any longer. You are imagining what is happening right now on Earth; people *are awakening to themselves again.*

Living the new paradigm is tuning into what feels natural, intuitive, expansive and freeing *on the inside.* When we live in accordance with what is true for us, we feel empowered and strong and we live into new possibilities for ourselves.

This is what I believe loving ourselves really is about. This might appear strange to the modern world purely because of the level of severe disconnect we are in. Yet when we are living in this energetic vibrational stance, we positively affect others in ways we can never know. That is how powerful we are.

This is what our natural sovereignty over ourselves is. This is the freedom that is our birthright beyond the conditioned mind and the external world's conditioning.

This is not new knowledge. It is reconnecting to something we already know very deep down but which we have been disconnected from the design of the world's systems.

We are here to trailblaze our own authentic, and *what feels true for us,* path in life and a beautiful and stunning by-product is that our energy supports others to do the same on the subconscious level. THAT is how important you are on Earth. You are not a cog in the wheel.

Our body is an amazing instrument that helps us to free ourselves from the conditioned mind - and remember it is our body that we have been disconnected from all along our timeline - right back from our parents or caregivers telling us to stop crying (stop feeling) as children, to the beauty industry we dabble with as teens with its subtle narratives that our bodies need to be perfect, look a certain way, smell this way, to the medical model narratives we hear around the 'body attacking you' relating to various chronic dis-ease as we move through time-space. Whatever you think about this, the point at hand is to reconnect with your amazing body because it is a route into freeing you from your conditioned mind. What is important is what YOU believe about it because whatever you believe about your body will be true for you.

Living into the Vision

The new paradigm is closer than you think. It is within You and not 'out there'.

It does not belong to any authority outside of us. It is not in technology. It is not in legislation. It is not in retail therapy. It is not voting for people we know nothing about to make important decisions for us as a collective. It is not in politics.

It is not in the news agencies owned by the super wealthy that contribute to mass manipulation. It is not from those who begin wars to profit for their own ends. It is not from legalised educational systems that restrict true, child-led learning. It is not in religion. It is not from the industries that perpetuate the non-natural or violence as being normal. It does not lie in this group, or that movement, or that culture.

No, it comes from within ourselves, is concerned with powerful heart based existence and expanding consciousness to live our full potential.

The new paradigm is us; transforming the quality of the relationship we have to ourselves so we know our truth - who we really are beyond our conditioning and in turn, transforming the quality of connection we have to others from this energetically expansive space.

The 'by-product' is we begin to see when others are in their patterns, and we can hold compassion for them rather than blame and judgment. Our change in our energy field gives them the green light to change who they are on the subconscious level. This is how powerful we are to each other. We modern humans are learning (reconnecting) more and more our potential as energy Beings.

Something amazing occurs when we start to focus our attention within ourselves, our inner space, when we are able to be with ourselves in stillness – even the painful parts of ourselves. We become calmer, more neutral, and increase our ability to respond and not react. We plug directly into Life Source, Creator, God, One Mind (there are many ways to express this connection).

I believe we naturally, deep down, know that paradigms that promote competition, separation, conflict, and division are not what we are about. We must learn to trust ourselves again rather than placing trust unconsciously in external worldly systems. Your body systems will always tell you what is true for you. We need to learn to feel into them. And the more we clear our patterns, the more obvious this becomes.

It is like looking at the world through a sparkling clean window, and once you see through it, you cannot forget the clarity once you have seen it.

This is how we shape our future, the world's future. The future on Earth is where the sacredness of humanity and Nature are deeply valued. It is a future full of cooperation, support, encouragement and celebration to be here.

It is already here now if we choose to believe it and live it.

Note by the lead author

Ramona really gets straight to the heart of what living in the new paradigm actually means…and that is to live from a heart centred perspective, free from believing the lies perpetuated by the few to create fear keeping us all subservient.

She describes how many of the beliefs we carry around with us are not our own, rather we inherit them from our caregivers, or they form based on what goes on in our environment and by the stories we hear.

Ramona asks to learn to trust ourselves again and to disconnect from fear laden mainstream media. The more of us that do this, the more of us who learn to recognise the lies designed to hold us in fear, the more of us who simply choose to STOP believing all we are told – the faster we will all reach the new paradigm.

Like Nikki and Natasha, she urges us to look deep inside, and asks us to seek out our inner child, the very essence of ourselves, and tell them they are safe, cared for, and need not live in a place of fear. By doing so, we will heal ourselves and raise our personal energetic frequency. This high level frequency can then be directed out into the world to help others find their way through and into a new way of living.

There are many quotes I could pull from Ramona's work. This one stands out: "Your body systems will always tell you what is true for you. We need to learn to feel into them. And the more we clear our patterns, the more obvious this becomes. It is like looking at the world through a sparkling clean window, and once you see through it, you cannot forget the clarity once you have seen it."

Chapter 10

Dreaming of a Better Future

by William (Bill) Baker

Deciding to take advantage of the company rule that those who worked longer hours in winter could knock off early in summer, at 11 am John switched off his computer, said goodbye to his friends, and left the office.

The sun was shining bright and warm, and a gentle breeze was blowing through the clean streets. John decided to take a walk down the avenue of lime trees that he had always admired; the trees were tall and elegant, with a lush canopy of green leaves that provided ample shade from the sun. Beyond it lay the green belt and a pleasant walk home.

John has lots to be grateful for: a loving family, loyal friends, a good job and a well governed, vibrant and outward looking community in which to live and grow.

Consensus is a key element in the decentralised system of government that runs the country; decisions are reached through a process of dialogue and negotiation among stakeholders. Communities have a greater say in the policies that affect their daily lives rather than having decisions made for them by distant and detached government officials. Procedural secularism allows for a diversity of perspectives to be heard and taken into account and for decisions to be made that reflect the interests and needs of all members of the community.

Those motivated by ambition for the power of high office are denied it; the country is run by people who are genuinely interested in the lives of the people they serve and who are competent judges of the issues that need to be resolved.

John was happy with many of the enlightened decisions the government had made. The town was clean, efficient, and walkable, with ample green spaces and public transportation that functioned to a high standard. The buildings are constructed with eco-friendly materials and powered by renewable energy sources. The air is clean, and the streets are quiet, as cars have been replaced by electric or autonomous vehicles. What vehicles there are cannot be parked on the roads or in front of houses; building regulations mean each road of houses has a neat and functional access road behind them, where the unsightly bins are also kept.

Work is no longer a burden or a source of stress, as technology has made it possible to automate many of the most tedious or dangerous jobs. Technology has advanced to the point where it is used to enhance the quality of life for all, rather than to exploit resources or increase inequality. People have the freedom to pursue their passions and interests, and work is viewed as a means of contributing to society rather than as a way to accumulate wealth or power. The only time the government can intervene in the liberty of the people is to stop someone from doing harm to another, but otherwise, individuals are free to pursue their own ends.

As he walked, John couldn't help but marvel at the beautiful and stylish Georgian houses that lined the street, one thankfully untainted by the horrors of modern architecture, which mercifully had proved to be a brief and passing phase. The houses are stately and grand, with intricate details and ornate facades.

John had always been fascinated by architecture, and he couldn't help but admire the craftsmanship and attention to detail that had gone into these buildings. It was pleasing to see a return to traditional crafts, which meant the manufacture of high quality goods, built to last.

The flowers that surround the trees and the houses add to the beauty of the scene, each homeowner considering their front garden a gift to the street; the flowers' sweet fragrance fills the air. John felt at peace as he walked, surrounded by the natural beauty of the world around him and a built environment that complemented it. He could walk along the road with his head up, admiring the landscape, because he knew the paving slabs would not present a trip hazard; the local council having an obligation to ensure that pavements, including sufficient lighting, are safe, and potholes are repaired promptly.

John's community is enhanced by an emphasis on sustainability. The towns and villages are all connected by a network of bike paths and pedestrian walkways, which wind their way through fields of wildflowers and rolling hills, and along crystal clear rivers teeming with trout. These paths and walkways are improved by the addition of publicly funded art installations and by clear signage.

The people here value community and collaboration above all else. There are community gardens and communal living spaces where residents can come together to grow food, share resources, and support each other. Local businesses thrive, and there is a focus on supporting the local economy and reducing waste.

The residents are deeply committed to protecting the natural world, and there are strict laws and regulations in place to ensure that the environment is preserved for future generations.

Rewilding schemes are in place, and biodiversity is encouraged; natural reserves and wildlife sanctuaries abound.

People live in harmony with each other and the natural world in a way that allows each individual to flourish. The residents have created a sustainable and supportive community that values creativity, collaboration, and environmental stewardship. Slowly but surely, there has been a shift in the way people view things. The aggressive Western dialectic, with its relentless pursuit of truth and progress, was imperceptibly being replaced by a softer, more cyclical Eastern way of interpreting the world. People work to find compromise, and accept the conflict of ideas; people can disagree without falling out with each other.

The excellent schools, with their small class sizes, are designed to foster creativity and a love of learning. Rote memorisation has been replaced with a focus on skills and the application of knowledge. Students are encouraged to explore their passions and interests, and the curriculum is focused on real-world problem-solving, critical thinking and emotional intelligence. The arts and humanities are celebrated and free from the unwelcome intrusion of scientism; no longer will the great works of fiction be subject to analysis from neuroscience or evolutionary biology. There is a real breadth of opportunity, so each individual can find their niche, and in schools, as in the wider community, there are plenty of opportunities for people to participate in sport, adventure, theatre, music, and visual arts. Local societies hold interesting talks which are open to all, and the residents are keen to hear from specialists in their particular field in order to gain a better understanding of the world around them.

At the end of the avenue John crossed over the road and climbed over a stile. After a short time, he noticed the gentle hum of a cricket match in progress in a small clearing.

With nowhere particular to be and nothing urgent to do, he sat down under one of the oak trees to watch a passage of play. He loved the sound of leather on willow, the rustling of leaves, and the distant bleating of sheep. Children ran around, playing tag and chasing butterflies in one of those never-ending days of youth.

The landscape is a patchwork of green fields, dotted with grazing sheep and cows and framed by gently rolling hills. It is here in the hinterland that the rewilding schemes are most evident. Reducing the human intervention characteristic of modern farming has allowed nature to take its course. The land has been allowed to become overgrown with vegetation, and large herbivores such as red deer and longhorn cattle have been reintroduced, as have more endangered species such as the purple emperor butterfly, turtle dove, and nightingale.

In the distance, a towering broach spire indicates a local village church nestled into the hillside. The church itself is made of ancient stone from a nearby quarry, and it has beautiful stained-glass windows. The chiming of the church bells adds to the bucolic ambience of the landscape. Like all places of worship, the church is a hub of multiculturalism, where people of all faiths and none come to share their experiences of the numinous. They engage in community activities and raise significant sums for local charities. They help to organise frequent community events with music and dancing, with stalls selling all manner of locally produced goods.

The economy is based on cooperation and sustainability. The emphasis is on local production and consumption, and there is a focus on reducing waste and minimising the impact on the environment; recycling centres are easily accessible, and the residents are happy with the expectation that everything that can be recycled is.

145

The concept of ownership has been redefined, and many goods and services are shared or leased rather than owned outright.

Social justice is also a core value, and everyone is treated with dignity and respect. Discrimination based on race, gender, or any other characteristic has been eliminated, and diversity is celebrated. Healthcare is free and available to all, and mental health is given as much priority as physical health.

In this place of timeless beauty, the simplicity of rural life is celebrated and cherished. It is a landscape that speaks to the soul, reminding us of the importance of nature, community, and leisure. The cricket match, against the backdrop of trees, hills, and the church with its majestic spire, is a beautiful reminder of the enduring traditions of rural England, where the passage of time is marked not by the clock but by the rhythms of the land.

Wokeness has been consigned to the past. It hadn't taken long for ordinary people to work out that the pernicious habit some people had of being too easily offended led to a culture of intolerance and censorship, which was not desirable. People can speak freely, though they are responsible for their words just as they are for their actions. There are no more echo chambers to reflect the closed mindedness of earlier times; free enquiry is promoted as vociferously as the emancipation of women, and tribalism has been consigned to history.

Things from the past are conserved irrespective of positive or negative connotations; lessons that needed to be learnt have been learnt and passed on to the next generation, and as a consequence, heritage industries thrive. For in this place the value of history is known, and the positive impact of community and continuity on the mental health of the people is reflected in the attitudes to the past.

This is a place of harmony and abundance; the natural world is revered and protected, and people live in harmony with the environment. Society is based on cooperation and collaboration rather than competition, and the well-being of all is considered more important than the wealth of a few.

John stepped over the threshold of his comfortable home and said, "Let there be light", and there was because all homes were smart homes, and voice activation was the new norm.

Note by the lead author

And so we end the chapters written by the adult collaborators the way we began – with a story. Bill's (William's) is written in the present tense, and I love that. He writes as if all the things he dreams of have already happened. And, as anyone who practices the law of attraction knows, setting intentions based in the here and now is essential.

A lot of the concepts I wrote about in my chapter – living in line with nature, tech taking over some jobs, a focus on community and sustainability – are present in Bill's section. Unlike my post-apocalyptic scenario, however, his seems to have morphed out of the old world. A much less destructive way of building a new future and an approach I hope and pray comes true!

I really like the way he has embraced the idea of keeping what feels like a traditionally British village way of life, complete with architecture from the past, as opposed to modern design. Aesthetically pleasing for sure (in the right context) but I hope his new world does allow for freedom of choice in where one lives and in what style of building one makes into a home. Although I am all for getting rid of vast urban metropolises!

"Society is based on cooperation and collaboration rather than competition, and the well-being of all is considered more important than the wealth of a few."

I think we can all agree that this is the mantra we should ALL be living by right now!

About the Authors

Laura Billingham – Lead Author

Laura is a multi-published author, with a historical novel and a compilation of short stories in her own name, as well as numerous contributions to other collaborative books and magazines.

She lives with her long-term partner in the beautiful Peak District in the UK and works as a ghostwriter and editor whilst also writing her own creations.

With one grandson and two more grandchildren on the way in 2024, any spare time is devoted to being the daftest granny on the planet.

Email: **hello@word-witch.co.uk**
Website: **www.word-witch.co.uk**
Book Website: **www.livinginthenewparadigm.com**

Amanda Cookson

Amanda is a professional coach working with founders, technical directors and leaders across the North. She is an NLP master practitioner and expert in conversational neuroscience which she uses to help clients elevate productivity and performance through conversations. Amanda co-founded her business Northern Value Creators with her husband Simon. They live in the Peak District with their 2 children, Vizsla, 2 guinea pigs and a rabbit.

Follow: **Amanda Cookson on LinkedIn**
Follow: **Northern Value Creators on LinkedIn**
Get free resources with the Juice her fortnightly newsletter:
https://www.northernvaluecreators.com/the-juice/

Andrea Hochgatterer

Andrea, originally from Austria, has, after a twenty-year stint as an artist in the UK film and entertainment industry, re engaged with her passion for all things health and healing.

Since 2005, Andrea has been working as a healing facilitator with clients from all over the world.

Continuing her voyage of discovery into all things weird and wonderful, she is keenly aware that the world we live in is changing and hopes that lending her voice through writing will positively influence those changes.

Contributor to collaborative books, lead author in her own published book "The Stress Maze", she is awaiting the publication of her first novel.

Email: **hochgatterera@aol.com**
Website: **www.mindbodyalignment.co.uk**

Beverly Radley

Beverly Radley is a beacon of light for those struggling in the chaos of life. She weaves together her roles as a healer, intuitive iCF Coach, author, and creative educator. With a culinary flair and a love for colour, she infuses creativity into every aspect of her work, appreciating the uniqueness and beauty in all living things. She shares her skills in workshops, retreats and conferences worldwide.

She now creates her own range of "Breakthrough From within" vibrational essences. Having trained with renowned essence makers Ian white, Ann Callaghan and Daniel maple. Beverly is determined to "Be the change she wants to see in the world."

Email: **Bevradley@gmail.com**
Instagram/Facebook: **Breakthrough from within**
LinkedIn: **Beverly Radley**
TikTok**: breakthroughbev**
For a free meditation, visit **SoundCloud**

Elke Wallace

Elke Wallace is a Performance Enhancement Specialist who helps peopleunderstand and get to know their unique brain design and how to optimise and maintain brain wellness.

As the fourth child of pre-WWII generation parents, she has always been interested in history, other cultures and the "workings of the world".

Losing two nieces at infant age following "health products" took her on a path to question, research and investigate what is going on beyond the surface of story headlines, seeking truth and finding alternatives that could improve the lives of others.

Email: **elkeawallace@gmail.com**
Website: **www.masteringyourmindmatters.com**
Membership: **agilemind.club**

Femke Williams

Femke is a Dutch born former Nurse, who's been in the UK since 1999.

She now owns Rosewood Wellbeing (nr Sheffield) as a Wellbeing Artist & Coach/Mentor - integrating natural therapies, fatigue recovery specialism and the Healing Arts (music, voice, movement and art).

With a focus on burnout prevention and trauma recovery, she helps others to cultivate self-care and self-love for embodiment and self-liberation. She believes that this will cause a positive ripple effect for our collective healing too.

Femke previously co-authored the books 'The Speaker's Journey Vol II (Amplifying Your Voice)", and "Menopause: What Nobody Talks About" .

Email: **femke@rosewoodwellbeing.co.uk**
Website: **www.rosewoodwellbeing.co.uk**

Natasha Shaw

Working as a Transformational Mentor. Tasha is a CEDR accredited Mediator, trained in Conflict Dispute Resolution. 20+ years as an Executive Business Facilitator & Coach, HeartMath certified. Qualified in Parent Coaching (London Parent Practice).

She has worked under the guidance of Suzy Miller (Integration Specialist), for 10+ years and now runs legacy-leadership.co.uk and is the founder of Unified Behaviour Dynamics at tashashaw.com.

Supporting unification of both your inner and outer worlds, cultivating your still point and reconnection back to your wider aspects and soulful layers. And continues to be a curious learner of life's experiences as an expression of thrive!

Email: **natasha.shaw@outlook.com**
Website: **www.tashashaw.com** – Unified Behaviour Dynamics

———

Nikki Baker

I work in the health and fitness industry as a Personal Trainer (8 years), and a Fitness Behaviour Change Coach (4 years). I am soon to qualify to teach face-yoga and as a yoga instructor.

Throughout my work, I have always advocated the importance of balancing our mental, emotional and physical selves to create an overall sense of connection and well-being.

It is because of this belief that I felt strongly drawn to being part of this written collaborative work.

Email: **nikkiinoz@yahoo.com**

Ramona Stronach

Ramona Stronach, founder of Tap Your Possible and Author, loves inspiring and enabling others to reconnect to themselves beyond their conditioning that creates struggle in life, and energetically open up to possibility.

She left her Social Work profession to follow an inner impulse to discover what was possible for her own life. Along the way, she met Emotional Freedom Technique and Matrix Reimprinting – extraordinary and transformational energy tools and discovered her greatest success; self-connection beyond the conditioning of her own negative beliefs – a growing adventure.

Ramona trained with Master Karl Dawson, EFT Founding Master, creator of Matrix Reimprinting, Hay House Author.

Email : **ramona@tapyourpossible.com**

William Baker

William Baker grew up in the New Forest, and went to school in Southampton. After time spent living in Lancashire, Leicestershire and Lincolnshire, he tired of the alliteration, so moved to Tokyo where he spent a very enjoyable 18 months.

Returning to Hampshire in his late 20s, he decided to swap one National Park for another, and he moved to a picturesque market town in the South Downs, where he still lives. He spends what spare time he has reading, playing sport, appreciating architecture, listening to music and enjoying family life.

Contributions from the younger generation

Perfect Paradise

By Emily Baker, Age 9

Imagine a world where you could go anywhere you wanted. Where you could eat anything you liked and it would all be healthy. There would be no burglars but lots of burgers, and everything was perfect for everyone.

Apart from for one little girl and her friend.

They liked everything was healthy but they missed their old adventures solving crimes and helping arrest criminals. So, they packed their bags, said goodbye to their families, and went where spacecraft would fly you back to any world you liked.

So they picked Earth and flew back to their proper homes.

A few hours later the boy said, "I wonder how much longer until we'll get there."…and as a matter of fact, he said it just as they were landing.

"Look!" shouted Emily, "we're here."

"Oh yeah!" exclaimed Finley.

Once they had landed, they hopped off the spacecraft and found their way back home. Fortunately, they were next door neighbours.

Luckily, Emily knew the code to the safe, so she put in the code (1405791) and…it opened.

They found stacks and stacks of money and jewels. Since their homes were quite empty, they decided to go shopping for furniture and food.

So, they decorated their houses, and they were ready for their next adventure.

Voice of a teenager

By Hannah Pogson, Aged 16

Our world is a flower, blooming constantly, creating new inventions and expanding our knowledge about our life, and flourishing, creating a new view on life. However, it is hard to maintain and can easily become infected and poisoned, this is why we need to take care and make sure we protect it, even if that means fighting for our flower.

New generations are constantly being infected by the society we built, especially teenagers. Due to advances in technology, new concepts of how a person should be have been created. Even though we have evolved from the classist and patriarchal society, many ideologies are still being used today, especially women in society, but due to social media many children and teens are being criticised for not only their looks but also their intelligence. It has become a crime to make mistakes and our education system is contributing to that. Children are developed into introverted, afraid machines that are used to contribute to our economy, this is due to avarice in our world.

Our world has injected fear into young children, and it is ripening every day. We are told that to get wealthy you need to follow the education system: go to school, college, and university, but this leads to a standardised society.

School teaches children that you cannot make mistakes because mistakes lead to wrong answers, which leads to low test results, which ultimately leads to not getting a wealthy job.

This instils fear into younger generations and strips their creativity and innovation away, conforming them to a society that we tried so hard to get out of.

Social media and society are infecting one another; they are corrupting innocent children and teenagers due to their harmful nature. The concept of convergence and the internet is extraordinary. We can interact with family and friends, buy things and sell things with one button. However, that means that it is only one button to completely destroy someone.

Mental health for children and teens has risen to 1 in 6 from 1 to 9 in 2017 and mental health in children is declining every year. I am 16 and I worry that younger generations are at risk of taking a dark path, due to new trends. We need to take action, and this doesn't mean taking your child's phone off them, we need to help society build a new leaf, to bloom a new flower, one that is not avaricious or judgemental, but that is welcoming and safe; we need to have more protection online, especially on social media, to not let someone's life be taken away with one click, to not let stupid trends like 'legging legs' become a thing.

We need to teach the younger generations that beauty is in everything and everyone and that no amount of filters or makeup is going to affect that, and when we start building a safe society that isn't fuelled by hate then and only then can we start living in a new paradigm.

Conclusion

The co-authors and I hope you have enjoyed delving into our thoughts and musings on what we consider to be a new paradigm way of living.

Every one of the authors has a different take on the question of "what is a new paradigm way of living", and yet, as I mentioned in the intro, they all have a common denominator…

LOVE

Love of oneself, love of others, love of the planet, of nature, of the cosmos.

If we are to stand a chance of making this world a better place, it is up to all of us to raise the energetic vibrations of humanity to the highest frequency there is - love. Are you with us?

Collaborate

Would you like to feature in a second edition of Living in the New Paradigm?

Would you like to share your ideas and view point?

If the answer is YES please contact me:
hello@word-witch.co.uk

You can also find me on LinkedIn:
https://www.linkedin.com/in/laura-billingham-ghostwriter/

And here is the website where updates about the book(s) will be featured: www.livinginthenewparadigm.com

References

(Chapter 3 – Andrea Hochgatterer)

Science Nordic, violent knights feared post-traumatic stress, Kristian Sjorgen, translated by Michael de Laine.
The New Antiquity: Combat Trauma and the Ancient Greeks.
Peter Meineck, David Konstan, Combat Trauma and the Ancient Greeks. The New Antiquity. New York: Palgrave Macmillan, 2014. xiv, 310. ISBN 9781137398857
Smithsonian Magazine, Edward Watts.
Info taken from Psych Central, Biological Psychiatry, PUBmed. Bernd Steinbock, University of Western Ontario. bsteinbo@uwo.ca
PUBMed Central.
Jennifer C. Chan,1 Bridget M. Nugent,2 and Tracy L. Bale2 Author information Copyright and License information Disclaimer
Taken from Archetypes, 1982 Dr Anthony Stevens.

(Ramona Stronach – Chapter 9)

Gregg Braden, Human By Design, 2017
Gregg Braden, Wired To Thrive, The Sixth Truths of Extraordinary Living, Online Course,
www.hayhouse.com, 2016
Karl Dawson, Kate Marillat, Transform Your Beliefs, Transform Your Life, 2014
Dr Joe Dispenza, Breaking the Habit of Being Yourself, 2012
Shakti Gawain, Living in the Light, 1998
David Hamilton, How you can Heal your Body, 2008
Sir David Hawkins, The Map of Consciousness Explained, 2020

Esther Hicks, Jerry Hicks, The Law of Attraction, 2006
Peter Levine, In an Unspoken Voice, 2010
Lester Levenson, Hale Dwoskin, Happiness is Free, 2020
Bruce Lipton, The Biology of Belief, 2005
Lynne McTaggart, The Field, 2003
Dr Sue Morter, The Energy Codes, 2019
Eckhart Tolle, A New Earth, 2005
John Vibes, Derrick Broze, Finding Freedom in an Age of Confusion (The Conscious Resistance), Volume 2, 2016

Printed in Great Britain
by Amazon

44012995R00096